Ferruccio Canali

The Basilica of
SANTA CROCE

Under the Patronage of the **Società di Studi Fiorentini**

180 color photographs
plan of the monumental complex of Santa Croce

BONECHI
edizioni il Turismo
FIRENZE-1954

PLAN OF THE MONUMENTAL COMPLEX OF SANTA CROCE

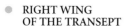

RIGHT WING OF THE TRANSEPT

A Castellani Chapel
B Baroncelli Chapel

MONASTERY WING

C Corridor
D Sacristy
E Rinuccini Chapel
F Monastery Wing or Novitiate
G Chapel of the Novitiate, or of the Medici

CHAPELS AT THE END OF THE TRANSEPT

H Velluti or San Michele Chapel
I Calderini or Riccardi Chapel
J Giugni or Bonaparte Chapel
K Peruzzi Chapel
L Bardi Chapel
M Main Chapel
N Tolosini or Spinelli Chapel
O Benci or Capponi Chapel
P Ricasoli Chapel
Q Bardi di Libertà or Pulci-Beraldi Chapel
R Bardi Chapel or Chapel of St. Silvester
S Niccolini Chapel

LEFT WING OF THE TRANSEPT

T Bardi Chapel (di Vernio)
U Salviati Chapel or Chapel of San Lorenzo

I Main Cloister
II Museo dell'Opera di Santa Croce
III Second Cloisteror Large Cloister
IV Pazzi Chapel

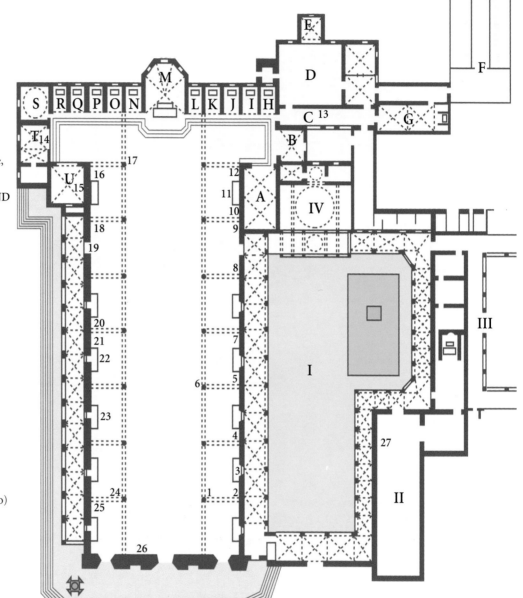

1. Madonna del Latte
2. Monument to Michelangelo
3. Ascent to the Calvary (Vasari)
4. Cenotaph to Dante
5. Monument to Vittorio Alfieri
6. Pulpit (Benedetto da Maiano)
7. Monument to Niccolò Machiavelli
8. Annunciation (Donatello)
9. Tomb of Leonardo Bruni
10. Tomb of Gioacchino Rossini
11. Christ's Entry into Jerusalem (Cigoli)
12. Tomb of Ugo Foscolo
13. Monument to Lorenzo Bartolini
14. Wooden Crucifix (Donatello)
15. Tomb of Sofia Zamoyska
16. Monument to Raffaello Morghen
17. Monument to Leon Battista Alberti
18. Monument to Carlo Marsuppini
19. Organ
20. Pietà (Bronzino)
21. Monument to Angelo Tavanti
22. The Incredulity of St. Thomas (Vasari)
23. Supper at Emmaus (Santi di Tito)
24. Tomb of Galileo
25. Fresco Cycle (Mariotto di Nardo)
26. Monument to Gino Capponi
27. Crucifix (Cimabue)

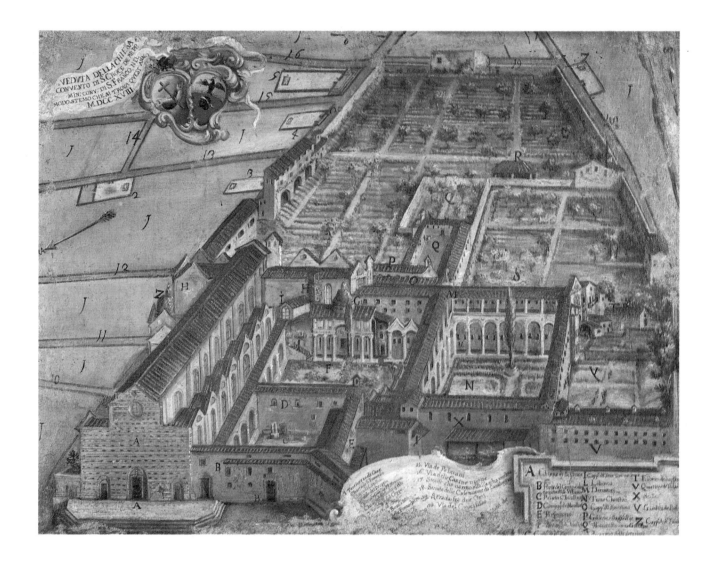

THE MONUMENTAL COMPLEX OF SANTA CROCE

● HISTORICAL NOTES

The first church of Santa Croce, was much smaller than the existing one. The remains of the early church were discovered after the last flood that struck Florence, and can be seen by going down the stairs in the left nave. It was built in an area that is lower than the nearby city center, and hence subject to disastrous floods (in 1966, the floodwaters rose to a height of 4 meters). In fact, in earlier times, the area was occupied by a small island and a branch of the Arno River which dried up. Around 1220 the Franciscans selected this spot for a monastery, in a poor district where there was probably a small oratory. It was a growing district, with not many inhabitants just outside the second circle of walls (1173-75) that stood on what is now Via dei Benci and Via Verdi. By 1252 the new church was completed, and although it was much smaller than the existing one (it was about as wide as the left nave and outside portico, and as long as the first five "bays" we can see today) it had the same Egyptian cross plan (that is, the transept is at the end of the longitudinal narthex) with chapels on the back wall. Compared with the

Above: *the monumental complex of Santa Croce in a painting dated 1718.*

3

Dominicans' church of Santa Maria Novella that was built during the same period and which soon became the center of orthodox Christianity against the expanding heresies, the monastery of Santa Croce became a place for the faithful to gather and discuss doctrine through the stories told in paintings (the great didactic or educational painting cycles). However, the monastery soon became the driving force in the city's life. In its district it promoted population growth and as it also comprised confraternities, it involved the lay population through daily and weekly charity as well as a whole series of crafts industries..

In 1262 a large lot was purchased to enlarge the original church, and in 1294 as noted in Villani's Chronicles, "on the day of the Holy Cross in May, the new church of the Friars Minor of Florence, known as Santa Croce, was established...And they began the foundations at the rear, where the chapels are because first there was the old church, for the friars' offices, and finally the new chapels were built."

The design has been attributed, at least starting from Vasari, to Arnolfo di Cambio the famous architect who built many important buildings in the city such as Palazzo Vecchio and the Cathedral of Santa Maria del Fiore (1296). With major financing from the city, Arnolfo designed a basilica with three naves; the central and largest of the naves higher than the others, and three doors. When the architect died in 1302 the end part of the choir and chapels were all that had been completed, but by 1320 the new church was almost completely functional and it was finished (except for the façade) in 1385. However, the church was only dedicated in 1443, by Cardinal Bessarione in the presence of Pope Eugenius IV. It is likely that Leon Battista Alberti, a member of the pope's entourage, was present (we must not forget that the central chapel -which is now the choir - belonged to the Alberti family in the fourteenth century). Even though the building still had no façade, the rough stone had already been decorated with the large plaque of Saint Bernardino, the initials IHS surrounded by rays, which, along with Donatello's statue of *St. Louis of Toulouse*, that was placed in a niche above the door, sanctioned the building's full involvement in the new, Humanistic cultural current. In fact, the fifteenth century marked the moment of maximum expansion for the entire Santa Croce complex, with a series of renovations and embellishments inside, and the rebuilding of the monastery wings after a disastrous fire that struck in 1423. The renovations culminated in the construction of the wing known as the Noviziato by Cosimo and Piero de'Medici; starting around 1440, the monastery library and the large cloister, and then with the construction of the Pazzi Chapel that lasted until 1461.

In 1504 public financing came to a halt, and once again work on the façade was postponed. It was only in the second half of the sixteenth century, thanks to renewed interest in the building on the part of the Grand Duke Cosimo that the interior was remodeled, and then work began on the new bell tower in 1551 only to be interrupted shortly thereafter. In the following centuries work was only done on individual tombs and chapels.

In the nineteenth century, on the wave of the Romantic movement and the taste for celebrating Italian glory, the Santa Croce complex once again became a focal point in city life, first in the Lorraine dynasty celebrations, and then in the context of Florence as capital of the United Italy. Finally, the new bell tower, designed by Gaetano Baccani in 1842, the construction of the façade and the creation of the "Tempio delle itale glorie", with the tombs of Italy's great men were the two salient episodes that profoundly changed the interior and exterior appearance of the basilica which definitively became one of the greatest monuments in Florence and all of Italy.

THE PIAZZA

The activities of the Dominican, and Franciscan orders were fundamental in the urban development of Florence during the thirteenth century. As opposed to the other religious orders that established themselves in the city during the previous century, the Franciscans, in particular, were "urban", they chose the city and not nearby isolated areas like the Benedictines. The construction of their monasteries brought about profound changes in the appearance of the city, as large piazzas were created in front of them, and they became the headquarters for specific business activities and markets. After 1220 Piazza Santa Croce became an urban ambient closely tied to the Franciscan church. In addition to being a new trading or business center, and more generally a center for community life, it was also the site of outdoor sermons for crowds much larger than the original church could accommodate. Games and tournaments were held in the piazza starting in the fourteenth century, such as the tournaments of Lorenzo and Giuliano de' Medici in 1469 and 1475, and then the yearly Calcio Storico (historic football) matches began in 1530.

Above: *the façade;* opposite: *statue of Dante Alighieri,* by Enrico Pazzi.

View of Piazza Santa Croce;
below, from the left: *detail of
the façade of the Palazzo
dell'Antella and the fountain.*

The square that was originally flanked by poor dwellings of the lower classes, was gradually transformed as the Santa Croce complex gained in importance. Thus, the *Palazzo Cocchi Serristori* (n. 1 opposite the basilica), believed to have been designed by Giuliano di Sangallo (1469-74) was rebuilt, and likewise the *Palazzo dell'Antella* (on the right side of the square) by Giulio Parigi with the large façade that was frescoed in only twenty days sometime between 1619 and 1620. In the XVII century, by order of the grand duke, the entire square was refurbished with benches and markers for barriers in pietra serena. In 1816 the fountain in front of Palazzo Cocchi was built to a seventeenth century design, and in 1865, the sculptor Enrico Pazzi placed the colossal statue of *Dante* in the middle of the square. In 1972, six years after the disastrous flood of 1966, the statue was moved to the left side of the parvis.

Print showing the nineteenth construction of the façade; below: model of the façade, to plans by Nicolò Matas.

THE NINETEENTH CENTURY FACADE

Like the cathedral of Santa Maria del Fiore and the church of San Lorenzo, in the mid-nineteenth century, the basilica of Santa Croce had a rough façade. It had not been completed due to the extreme delicacy inherent in the completion of the building, the frequent lack of money for such a costly undertaking, the changes in taste and artistic canons and the impoverishment Florence suffered from the XIV to the XVIII century. Thus, in the nineteenth century Santa Croce was still characterized by the toothing in the never-completed parament: on the front with a single spire there was a large, oculus closed with stained glass designed by Ghiberti; above it a pietra serena tondo with the San Bernardino plaque and the Christogram that was added in 1437 after a plague epidemic; and below, the three entrances framed by pointed arches, of which the middle one was the highest. In 1469 Donatello's statue of St. Louis was placed in a niche above the main door, but in 1476 the problem of finishing the façade was vigorously brought up before the city authorities who ordered a design, probably by Cronaca, for the façade. Only a marble band on the lower right was completed, and then it was removed in the XIX century.

When, in the nineteenth century Santa Croce was elevated to the status of "National Pantheon" with the tombs or cenotaphs (that is funerary monu-

From the top: statue of the Virgin in the central aedicula on the façade two statues of archangels on the spires of the left door.

ments, without the remains of the deceased) of the greatest Italians, once again the need was felt to complete the outside of the church according to the canons of a decorous restoration in the old style. In 1854 all the decorations and paraments that had been added to the façade over the centuries were removed. Starting in 1837 the architect Nicolò Matas and the sculptor Lorenzo Bartolini had submitted plans in a late Gothic-Renaissance style to the Grand Duke Leopold, in an attempt to achieve a stylistic alignment with the interior of the basilica and a revaluation of the most glorious "Italic" roots. A few years later, in 1842 Matas was also commissioned to design a façade for the cathedral of Santa Maria del Fiore, and the polemics that arose after he submitted his first design for the cathedral convinced him of the need to study and redraw his plans for Santa Croce, not in a generic Gothic style, but in a language that was closer to the uniquely Florentine fourteenth century tradition. Having avoided a competition such as the ones being held at that time for the cathedral (in which Matas was defeated by De Fabris), the architect was pressingly asked "not to imagine but to discover, or guess" the idea that Arnolfo di Cambio would have wanted in the XIV century "abdicating all individual sentiment...but satisfying himself with reflecting the light - as a humble satellite - of the main star [that is, Arnolfo]." Obviously, this was not easy for Matas, who having seen the *empasse* of the situation he could not extricate himself from, after the flood that had submerged the complex in 1844, affirmed that in the basilica archives he found the old plans by Simone Pollaiolo known as Cronaca. These plans immediately disappeared again, and Matas said that he had only had the time to make a single copy. Although his contemporaries were obviously very suspicious of the entire story and hardly believed in his lucky discovery, Matas' design managed to convince even the greatest skeptics who wanted Santa Croce to have his façade. In August 1857, Pope Pius IX, on a visit to Florence, laid the first stone. Part of the project was also to revive the artisan spirit of the Florentine Renaissance workshops, especially when it came to defining and laying the green-white marble blocks, that were typical of the Florentine Medieval language. All the greatest sculptors in the city, and even the best students of the Accademia di Belle Arti were summoned by Matas to participate in the project with other sculptors: from Michelangelo Migliarini who, as organizer of the "Gallery of Statues" (Uffizi), gave his historical consulting to Aristodemo Costoli professor at the Accademia; from Ippolito Giorgi to Luigi Fabrucci; from Francesco Giovannozzi to Enrico Pazzi to the most famous Gaetano Bianchi and Giovvani Duprè, the most renowned, albeit controversial Florentine sculptor between 1840 and 1880.

The façade was officially inaugurated in April 1863 in the presence of Prince Emanuele di Savoia and many outstanding local citizens. Only Matas was absent, tired from the work, and annoyed by a bitter argument with Giovanni Duprè. All the critics, starting with Adolfo Venturi expressed their satisfaction with the work, and mainly with the reliefs carved by Duprè.

In 1865 the façade was finally completed on the occasion of Dante's sixth centennial and the transfer of Italy's capital to Florence. The statue of Dante was placed in the middle of the square (now it is on the left side of the parvis), and the famous bas-reliefs by Giovanni Duprè were placed in the lunettes above the three doors.

DESCRIPTION

The façade of the basilica of Santa Croce - one of the most significant episodes in late XIX century artistic sensitivity and taste as expressed by the desire of the builders and craftsmen to complete the Medieval building in a late Gothic/Renaissance style - was built with the cooperation of some of the finest Florentine architects, sculptors and art experts of the latter half of the period. On the basis of the alleged sixteenth century designs by Cronaca, the façade was embellished with a tricuspidate termination, below which the architectural parts were resolved with a close network of white and green Carrara marble panels in the Medieval Florentine tradition. The front was decorated only by the addition of the three great doors decorated with relief sculptures; rows of arches (at the height of the roof of the lateral naves and the central nave) and then by the spires on the sides of the three cusps and the doors. This tight rhythm was created by in-depth geometric and proportional studies, and it unites the Medieval structure of the basilica with the nineteenth century façade thanks to Matas' intent to continue the architectural mood of Arnolfo di Cambio's and Cronaca's designs.

A series of inlays enliven the rigid structure of the two-colored panels. In particular, the band at the top of the highest central door, with its rhombus-shaped geometric designs, is closely related to the panels on the Romanesque church of San Miniato al Monte, Giotto's bell tower for the cathedral and the Alberti's façade on the basilica of Santa Maria Novella. Even the six-pointed star in the large central tympanum at the top, closing the median part of the entire façade, is purely Medieval, notwithstanding the design with the rays (St. Bernardino's plaque) in the center which is a fifteenth century motif.

There are many relief sculptures. In the tondos on the four pillars at the end of each nave are depictions of the *Doctors of the Church: St. Augustine, St. Jerome and St. Bonaventure.*

Giovanni Duprè carved the *Our Lady of Sorrows* which is on the baldachin above the central door, known as the door of *the Redeemer.* But the idea of placing it inside the aedicula was not the best, and by 1872 Duprè was complaining that the statue seemed smothered, and the aedicula resembled a "candle snuffer".

Above, left: *disc and tympanum of the façade and the plaque of St. Bernardino;* below: *statues of archangels on the spires of the right door;* opposite: *the right door.*

9

Preceding page: *the façade of Santa Croce.*
Above: *Exaltation of the Cross,* by Giovanni Duprè;
below: *Invention of the Cross,* by Tito di Sarocchi.

In the intrados of the main door, there is a series of works by Luigi Fabruzzi and Francesco Giovannozzi, while the central lunette is embellished the *Exaltation of the Cross*, by Duprè. This artistically significant marble relief was praised by critics of the caliber of Adolfo Venturi and Alfredo Melani, who said that it revealed "the soul, faith and genius of Duprè to their fullest extent", in his attempt to create not only an abstract representation but also a rather natural portrayal of the figures (in addition to the reproposition of the figurative schemes of Beato Angelico and Raphael).

In the left door, known as the door *of the Patriarchs,* the panels with the busts were carved by Giuliano Chiari, while the lunette with the *Invention* (or finding) *of the Cross,* by Tito Sarocchi of Siena, was dictated as an iconographic motif by Duprè himself. He asked that "the cross be raised from below the ground by three strong men, in the presence of Helena and her handmaids...but without too much symmetry."

The reliefs on the right door, known as the door of the Prophets, because of their portrayals, were done by Enrico Pazzi, while, following Duprè's advice, Emilio Zocchi carved the Apparition of the Cross for the lunette. The jambs of the three doors are decorated with reliefs, known as candelabra, in a definite neo-fifteenth century style.

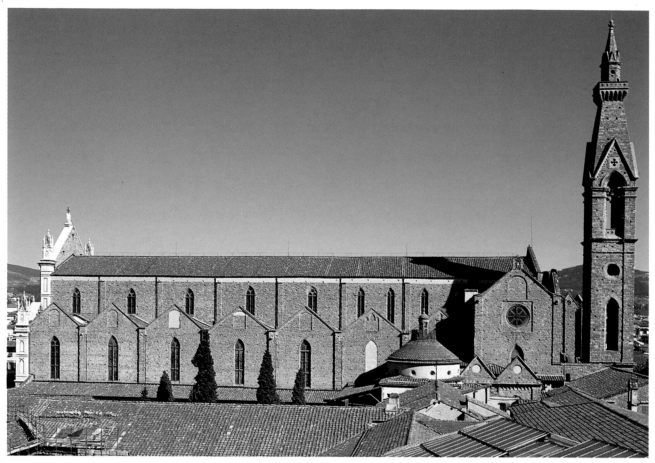

South side of the basilica, and the nineteenth century bell tower; below: *detail.*

THE BELL TOWER

The basilica's bell tower was only built in 1842 by the architect Gaetano Baccani, following a series of vicissitudes. In 1512 a bolt of lightning demolished the old structure that had been in precarious condition since at least 1462. Although work on the construction of a new bell tower, designed by Francesco da Sangallo, son of the famous Giuliano, on the left side of the façade had started in 1551, it remained unfinished until the XIX century, and on the right side of the rear of the basilica, where it still stands today. Baccani was particularly aware of the Gothic architecture in the city, and he reproposed it in updated form in his designs. In fact, for the Santa Croce bell tower he studied the structure of fourteenth century Florentine bell towers. Baccani's interpretation of the new bell tower - that was constructed amidst many difficulties because it rests on the walls of the Medieval chapels, and much criticism on the part of the powerful architect Pasquale Poccianti who opposed "Neo-Gothic barbarism" - fully shows the architect's ability to re-elaborate famous models, reducing the traditional registers from four to three, simplifying the windows by making them single-lighted, and adding a rather unusual, but well-set spire.

Central nave;
below: *Crucifix* by the
"Maestro di Figline",
in the Main Chapel.

THE INTERIOR

The interior of the basilica is a typical example of the Italian Gothic, and mainly of the version that was developed by the begging orders such as the Franciscans. It is a very subdued Gothic, without soaring decorations, with a large central nave that could hold a large number of faithful. It is characterized by a simple, trussed wooden ceiling which, as Vasari recalls, "Arnolfo designed a church with a large central nave and two smaller ones, and with much wisdom, not wanting to build vaults beneath the roof because it was so big, built arches from pillar to pillar, and above them a roof with a pediment", that is like a shed with visible beams that were restored many times over the centuries. Thus, the Gothic language in Santa Croce does not come through so much in the structure of the big, pietra forte octagonal pillars (since the more typical Gothic pillars are usually quite complex and clustered as in the large capitals that are divided into two, fourteenth century types: the "foglie d'acqua" that is, with very simple elongated leaves as on the first pillar on the right; and the "Corinthian" leaves, a Medieval version of the ancient classical models, as on the second pillar on the right.
Above the capitals are wide, pointed arches between the pillars, and they

Preceding page: *areas in the transept;* above: *grave markers in the floor.*

are, indeed, typically Gothic. Immediately above the keystone of the arches (their highest geometric point), there is a walkway along the walls of the central nave. Like the band that structured Early Christian basilicas, this highlights the upper part of the wall known as the cleristory, which is opened by a series of big windows.

Near the end of the church the walkway rises abruptly, with a flight of steep steps, thus highlighting the access to the two lateral wings of the transept which thereby become autonomous space with respect to the overall structure of the complex.

Before the sixteenth century, the area of the main nave did not resemble what we see today. There was a wall below the upper walkway, that closed off the central nave making it impossible to see the choir (which is visible today), and this emphasized the relative independence of the terminal part from the naves. That wall, which then went around the pillars (at the bottom of the fifth one on the left and right we can still see the base where those dividing walls were attached), was crowded by a series of chapels that were probably treated as altars, thus creating a totally autonomous, "private" section in the final part of the basilica.It was a real tribune up against the main body of the naves, with a sort of visual filter between the choir area and the worshippers. Giorgio Vasari's sixteenth century designs, in line with the dictates of the Counter Reformation, imposed that the division be eliminated and that the Sacrament be visible to all those present in the church. This had never been the case before. Thus the terminal dividing walls were taken down, and Arnolfo's original plans were profoundly modified. In the choir Vasari built a large gilded altar with the ciborium with a large cupola so that it would be the visual fulcrum of the entire basilica (the altar was later dismantled).

Finally, we must mention the floor, which is made of Florentine cotto tiles. It is dotted with a large number of grave markers, dating from the XIV to the XVIII centuries, many of which have been worn down by the countless visitors who walk over them.

Two angels, details of the stained glass windows in the Main Chapel; below: *Elijah and the Chariot of Fire,* by Giotto.
Opposite page: *stained glass window with Saints Cosma and Damiano,* the protectors of the Medici family,
by Alessio Baldovinetti, in the Chapel of the Novitiate.

STAINED GLASS WINDOWS

The stained glass windows in the lateral naves of Santa Croce are extremely interesting. The twenty-four windows were made between the XIV and XV centuries by the same artists who decorated the church walls with frescoes. The oldest ones are in the chapels and the upper part of the transept, closing the three oculi of the choir with Scenes from the Life of St. Francis. They were supposedly made after cartoons by Giotto, but it is more likely that the drawings were done by one of his pupils and Taddeo Gaddi (fragments of others are in the Museo dell'Opera). Then, still in the choir are stained glass windows by Agnolo Gaddi, as well as those in the Baroncelli Chapel, while the solemn figures on the windows of the Bardi and Tosinghi-Spinelli chapels were almost certainly designed by Giotto. There is a fifteenth century oculus that Ghiberti made to enhance the still unfinished façade, while Alessio Baldovinetti made the windows in the Chapel of the Novitiate, as well as the portrayal of *Saint Andrew* in the Pazzi Chapel. There is also a series of fine fifteenth century windows by Luca Signorelli, Antonio del Pollaiolo as well as Granacci, one of Michelangelo's companions.

THE MADONNA DEL LATTE *or della Mandorla*

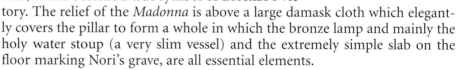

The relief sculpture on the first right hand pillar portrays the Virgin holding the Child inside a corona (known as the mandorla) of putti, in a typical mid-fifteenth century style which updates similar Medieval compositions. Because of the delicacy and grace that characterize the Virgin it can be considered typical of Antonio Rossellino's hand (however, it does not lack in similarity with works by another great sculptor of the period, Agostino di Duccio). The composition was done by Antonio, brother to the more famous Berdnardo Rossellino who collaborated with Alberti, within the context of the episodes of decorative updating which felt the influence of Albertian tastes that were already widespread since 1440. They were completed under Lorenzo the Magnificent following the Pazzi Conspiracy (1478). This monument was placed over the tomb of Francesco Nori, who was loyal to Lorenzo and was killed by the conspiracy. Thus, with its decorative lavishness, it also became a true symbol of Lorenzo's victory. The relief of the *Madonna* is above a large damask cloth which elegantly covers the pillar to form a whole in which the bronze lamp and mainly the holy water stoup (a very slim vessel) and the extremely simple slab on the floor marking Nori's grave, are all essential elements.

● *The wall of the right nave*

FIRST ALTAR

The altars that decorate the lateral walls of the basilica and which frame some fine paintings, are part of the furnishings that were added in the sixteenth century according to Giorgio Vasari's plans for architecturally embellishing the basilica's Medieval naves. It was done in a manner that favored the didatic cycles of paintings with respect to the frescoes on the walls that were mostly eliminated and of which a few traces remain. Each of these altars consists of "two large stone columns gracefully standing on dados", of capitals "carved with the subtle art of the Corinthian order", an architrave and then, as a crown a fronton which, in the course of the *suite* is either circular or triangular. These altars were originally connected by a continuous painted

Wall of the right nave.

cornice (two segments still remain on the sides of the *Monument to Michelangelo*). They contribute to rendering the rhythm of the church's architectural decoration very tight as they were added by Vasari to highlight the main altar he placed at the back of the church after having torn down the front wall of the choir near the Main Chapel to give the central nave a more monumental perspective. These grey pietra serena aediculae contain large canvases that tell the story of Christ's Passion according to a program created by Vicenzo Borghini, the great intellectual of the Medici court. These works were painted by the main artists from the Accademia Fiorentina del Disegno, thereby legitimizing the academy's role as the maximum force of court art, organized by the Grand Duke Cosimo de' Medici through the hands of Vasari and Borghini himself.

MONUMENT TO MICHELANGELO

The Monument to Michelangelo between the first and second altar was designed by Giorgio Vasari within the context of the 1570 renovations of the basilica. The sarcophagus is surrounded by allegorical figures of *Painting* (by Battista Lorenzi, who also carved the *bust* of Michelangelo which is above), of *Sculpture* (by Valerio Cioli) and of *Architecture* by Giovanni dell'Opera. The fresco with the *Pietà* is by Battista Naldini.
Next to Michelangelo's tomb is a series of sections of frescoes probably by Domenico Ghirlandaio that give an idea, albeit vague, of how the basilica's walls must have looked at the end of the fifteenth century before Vasari's renovations.

SECOND ALTAR

Here there is a canvas by Giorgio Vasari of the *Ascent to the Calvary*. The scene is crowded with characters and much motion in the gestures and garments to the extent that this painting is closer to Mannerism than the rigid Classicism that is so typical of Vasari's other works.

CENOTAPH TO DANTE

This cenotaph, erected by Stefano Ricci in 1829 was a response, to the never-fulfilled request to have the Poet buried in Florence. As early as 1396, the Republic of Florence had made the request to Ravenna, where Dante had died. However, once again the request went unheeded (it is important to recall Roberto Papini's interest in arranging Dante's tomb in Ravenna during the twentieth century). Although the cenotaph to Dante aroused the enthusiasm of many intellectuals, including Giacomo Leopardi who dedicated a song to the event, when the statue by Ricci, the finest Florentine interpreter of Canova's neo-classical lesson, was unveiled, disappointment and criticism abounded, although they were shrouded. It was said that Ricci who had been inspired by classical motifs, was culturally outdated with respect to the then fashionable revisitation of local culture and specifically the fifteenth and sixteenth century Florentine forms. One of the main points that drew criticism was the fact that Ricci had dressed the seated Dante in classical garments that were out of key with the Middle Ages, like the allegory of *Italy* that was also inspired by Canova's nearly forty-year old prototypes. On the other side, Poetry weeps for the death of the Poet that occurred in Ravenna in 1321.

MONUMENT TO VITTORIO ALFIERI

The work, a nodal point in the context of neo-classical sculpture and which attained wide renown throughout Europe, was commissioned by Luisa d'Albany who had been the poet's companion for nearly twenty years. It was carved by Antonio Canova in 1810, even though he had received the commission in 1803. Canova himself wrote that he had wanted to use a "as grave and majestic a style that was possible for me, in order to match the pride of this great poet's pen in the character of the sculpture", according to a classical principle that demanded the visualization of the soul in sculptural portrayals. Due to the general coldness found in Canova's works, (in fact, Roberto Longhi had defined him as "the sculptor who was born dead"), for many years the monument was not appreciated by the critics, although it was warmly received at its unveiling. However, it is in perfect in harmony with the neoclassical taste that straddled the XVIII and XIX centuries, of geometric abstraction and quest for pure form. As in the image of the mourning *Homeland* that renders tribute to Alfieri with the folds of the garment taken from ancient statuary, or in the general and great sobriety of the whole within which the only element that evokes forms with more motion, and it too is treated with great rigor, is the elliptical base of the monument.

24

PULPIT BY BENEDETTO DA MAIANO

The octagonal pulpit that stands against the third pillar of the main nave and which can be reached via a finely decorated inlaid door on the right nave was made by Benedetto da Maiano between 1472 and 1476. He used a vast repertory of elaborate decorative elements, and a marked polymateric taste that uses antique-ivory colored marble. Benedetto was commissioned by Lorenzo the Magnificent to create commemorative monuments in the cathedral of Santa Maria del Fiore; his idea was to create the structure for the stairs from a pillar in the basilica, this created more than a few perplexities for the workers of the Opera di Santa Croce due to the static problem which, in their opinion, would have been created by hollowing out a bearing wall. In the end, however, they proceeded with the work and enlarged the pillar. It was also made possible thanks to official financing by Piero Mellini, a patron who "did not look at costs, no matter how great". However, the lavishness of the decorations on the pulpit seemed to allude more to "court art"

Preceding page: *the Pulpit,* by Benedetto da Maiano. Above: *panel on the Pulpit portraying St. Francis Receiving the Stigmata;* above: *corner corbel of the Pulpit.*

Panel on the Pulpit portraying St. Francis Before the Sultan;
below: *sculpture* (like the classic Urania) in the bottom register of the pulpit.

than to a private commission. The panels contain bas-relief panels with Scenes from the *Life of St. Francis*, arranged according to the officially accepted version of the Saint's life. If from the figurative standpoint they seem to epitomize late fifteenth century taste for the representation of harsh scenes, as expressed by Pollaiolo or even Mantegna, from the setting standpoint they are extremely interesting, as Vasari noted, for having been carved with "trees, stones, houses, perspectives and several marvelous things", and from the architectural standpoint for the detail of the solemn hall shown in the *Confirmation of the Rule* (first panel on the left), or the magnificent palace of the Sultan of Babylon in the panel portraying *St. Francis Before the Sultan* (one of the best). Then come *St. Francis Receives the Stigmata, the Funeral of St. Francis* (with the typically humanistic capitals of the columns and basilica plan), *and the Martyrdom of the Early Fransicans.*

Monument to Niccolò Machiavelli by Innocenzo Spinazzi.

TANTO. NOMINI. NVLLVM. PAR. ELOGIVM
NICOLAVS. MACHIAVELLI
OBIT. AN. A. P. V. CIƆIƆXXVII.

MONUMENT TO NICCOLÒ MACHIAVELLI

This monument was made by Innocenzo Spinazzi in 1787. By the late nineteenth century, critics concurred in acknowledging the remarkable role he, who had come from Rome and had close relationships with transalpine artists, played in modernizing the late Baroque language of Florentine sculpture. The *Monument to Machiavelli* made by Spinazzi with the collaboration of other Florentine sculptors is certainly his most famous piece. It was commissioned after the republication of the statesman's sixteenth century works and the current of thought that developed thereupon. This tomb marks the apex of Spinazzi's adhesion to Enlightenment classicism, in the pose of the allegorical statue of *Politics* seated on the tomb, and carved after sixteenth century models, the classical lines of its face, and for the medallion-shield, treated like a cameo with the portrait of Machiavelli.

Preceding page: *Annunciation,*
by Donatello (as it is today).
Left: *corner relief with putti,*
originally on the aedicula
and now in the Museo di
Santa Croce;
below: *the aedicula before the
recent restorations.*

ANNUNCIATION BY DONATELLO
or Cavalcanti Annunciation

This tabernacle by Donatello was probably first placed in chapel - the Cavalanti Chapel which stood along Arnolfo's choir wall that was taken down by Vasari - along with Domenico Veneziano's panel portraying *St. Francis* and *St. John* (now in the Museo dell'Opera di Santa Croce). It was one of the most salient features of the fifteenth century renovations of the Medieval Basilica of Santa Croce. It is the fruit of the artistic period around 1435, that is after Donatello and Michelozzo broke up their artistic workshop. After the split Donatello made a second journey to Rome and came even closer to Leon Battista Alberti who was by now "a great friend". The relief of the *Annunciation* with the *Angel* on the left and the *Virgin* on the right, is framed by an aedicula enhanced with classical shapes and carvings which the critics in many ways have defined as being of Greek and Etruscan rather than Roman inspiration. This is also true for the lateral scaled pillars (perhaps based on those in the classic temple of the Fountains by Clitumnus) which do not rest on an ordinary base, and instead of the capital have four facing faces as found on many Etruscan earthenware vases from Chiusi. Even the idea of two figures in an aedicula is ancient and recalls the Greek stele or even Roman funerary aediculae, while on the sides of the crowning part, above, Donatello had planned on two groups of terracotta putti (that have since been removed and taken to the Museo dell'Opera) that were to have been based on the words of the ancient Roman architect Vitruvius who always recalled how the Etruscans used earthenware reliefs on the upper part of the temples. Even the soft folds of the figures' robes were described by the critics as being based on a series of classic models, while Donatello's ability to express states of mind with simple gestures (Mary's distress as she rises to her feet and turns her head) matches Giotto's frescoes in the basilica. The new Humanistic taste was also quite aware of the most significant examples of fourteenth century art, as in Giotto's works in Santa Croce (especially in the analytical and figurative attention the painter dedicated to Roman antiquities). In Donatello's tabernacle we must also note the winged garland in the bottom center, which is a clear sign of Leon Battista Alberti's sensitivity, as he was almost certainly involved in the search for all those stimuli that Donatello gathered from classic examples in designing this aedicula. One interesting fact emerged during the recent restorations to the tabernacle: white strips were found covering large parts of the aedicula after the removal of the white tempera which had been applied in the nineteenth century and up to now believed to have been original. Most probably, even originally, the white color was meant to simulate marble, thus, along with the gold color highlights, it ennobled the more common pietra serena.

TOMB OF LEONARDO BRUNI

Preceding page: *Tomb of Leonardo Bruni,* attributed to Rossellino's workshop. Left: *detail of the corner pilaster strip;* below: *frieze on the base of the Tomb of Gioacchino Rossini,* by Giuseppe Cassioli.

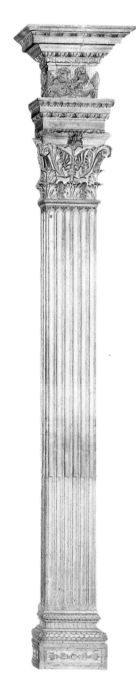

This is the first example of the humanistic tomb, perfectly structured according to fifteenth century sensitivities. It is a wall tomb treated as a closed aedicula with a semi-circular arched crowning part. After 1445-47 when Bernardo Rossellino built it the style rapidly became popular throughout the fifteenth century. Leonardo Bruni was the chancellor of the Florentine Republic from 1427 to 1444 and he wrote a monumental *History of the Florentine People.* He is portrayed in the relief stretched over the sarcophagus of his tomb in the garb of a rhetor, because of the great love and attention he had displayed for ancient Roman civilization throughout his life. The face, which is turned outward towards the viewer so that it can be readily seen from below - an unusual pose for the era - is finely detailed so that it is believed that the portrait was made from a true casting. The face was done by Antonio Rossellino, whereas the *Libro di Antonio Billi*, an early sixteenth century book dedicated to the lives of the artists mentioned Bernardno Rossellino, a collaborator of Leon Battista Alberti, as having done the composition of the whole. It is precisely to Alberti's world, Alberti was a friend of Bruni, that the design of this monumental complex is ascribed, if for no other reason than an entire series of formulas derived from the study of classical architecture. This also applies to the pilaster strips with grooves, that frame the central area containing the sarcophagus as well as the decorations on the capital with its tilted scrolls - a theme of which Alberti was particularly fond.

THE TOMB OF GIOACCHINO ROSSINI

This wall tomb was built in 1887 by the sculptor Giuseppe Cassioni. It is based on the nearby *Tomb of Leonardo Bruni*, in the climate of the neo-fifteenth century *revival* as regards the arrangement of the arcosolium (that is, a wall-tomb with an arch), with a typically nineteenth century addition of the praying figure. This was an innovation with the adaptation of a well-tried model to the new era and new sensibilities.

Preceding page: *Tomb of Gioacchino Rossini*, by Giuseppe Cassioli.
Left: *Christ's Entry into Jerusalem,* by Lodovico Cigoli; below: *Tomb of Ugo Foscolo,* by Antonio Berti.

SIXTH ALTAR

Here is a canvas by Lodovico Cigoli (1603-1604) of *Christ's Entry into Jerusalem*. In this painting the artist revealed how carefully he studied Titian's tonal lessons with his lively and profound use of various shades of color.

TOMB OF UGO FOSCOLO

The monument, in line with twentieth century sensibilities, is not a real tomb, but merely depicts the subject. It was made in 1939 by Antonio Berti, a spokesman of a classicism that, while adhering to academic tradition was simplified as to form, as we can see even from the dado base on which the figure rests.

Right: *Castellani Chapel;*
below: *detail of Scenes from
the Life of St. John the Baptist,*
by Agnolo Gaddi.

● *Right wing of the transept*

CASTELLANI CHAPEL

Going up the stairs that encircle the entire choir, on the left we come to the Castellani (or Santissimo) Chapel which was entirely frescoed with *Scenes from the Life of Saint Anthony, Saint John the Baptist, Saint John the Evangelist and Nicholas of Bari* by Agnolo Gaddi around 1385. In the XVIII century the walls were whitewashed because it was believed that such lavish wall decorations would distract from the liturgy and create too strong a contrast with the somber lines of the architecture, and only around 1870 was this fine fresco cycle uncovered.

On the right wall, in the first bay are the *Scenes from the Life of St. Nicholas,* and the *Scenes from the Life of Saint John the Baptist* are in the second. On the pillar between the two sectors there is a glazed terracotta of *Saint Francis,* made in the Della Robbia workshop sometime during the XV century.

On the back wall, to the left of the altar, are the Scenes from the *Life of St. Anthony Abbot,* which seems to have been done in 1385 by Gherardo Starnina, an artist who, albeit with a history and artistic production that are in many ways mysterious, came into contact with different stylistic tendencies during his travels to the extent that, in combination with the Giottoesque taste, he

The Temptation of St. Anthony Abbott, attributed to Gherardo Starnina;
below: *St. Francis,* glazed terra-cotta from the Della Robbia workshop.

became one of the most innovative painters who worked in Florence at the end of the XIV century. Then there is the *Crucifix* painted on a panel by Niccolò di Pietro Gerini, and beneath it, a XV century *Tabernacle* by Mino da Fiesole, with two pairs of angels in perspective flanking the doors of the aedicula. As a frontal, the altar has a carved relief with the *Marys of the Sepulchre* in the center, with two angels attending the arrival of the pious women, done by a pupil of Nicola Pisano in the XIV century. This is a significant piece on the panorama of fourteenth century Florentine sculpture because of the artist's attention to the references to classical reliefs as seen in some of the plasticism, and because it conveys the dramatic essence of the event and gestures, which is similar to the sensitivity of Nicola's son, Giovanni Pisano.

On the left wall of the chapel are other *Scenes from the Life of St. Anthony,* and near the entrance arch, *Scenes from the Life of St. John the Evangelist.* At the pillar which divides the two bays there is yet another XV century Della Robbia terra-cotta portraying *Saint Bernardino of Siena* who had preached in the basilica.

On the walls, on the lower part, there are some XIX century funerary monuments, such as the one dedicated to *Mikhail Skotnicki* (the first on the right) done in 1808 by Stefano Ricci, one of the Florentine artists who was most attentive to the neo-classical taste expressed by Canova who praised him highly.

A second, and highly interesting tomb monument is the one dedicated to *Luisa Stolberg, Countess of Albany* (left). This monument, dedicated to Vittorio Alfieri's companion was done in 1830 by Luigi Giovannozzi (decorations) and Emilio Santarelli (the statuary) to designs by the French architect, Charles Percier. Perfectly in line with the trend for recovering the fifteenth century traditions that had returned to the fore following the Restoration (1815), the tomb was immediately considered one of the best examples of the new trend, then known as "Tuscan Purism", that was born as a response to Neoclassicism. In particular, derived from fifteenth century works, in addition to the overall composition, it is mainly the winged genies who, without being overly naturalistic, eliminate that coldness which many attributed to contemporary neoclassical works.

BARONCELLI CHAPEL

Frescoed by Taddeo Gaddi from 1332 to 1338 when his teacher, Giotto, was still alive, the chapel has an interesting cycle with *Scenes from the Life of the Virgin,* from her birth to her death. The new datum in these portrayals is, without a doubt, the fact that they were done with a spirit that was less and less austere, up to representation of details from daily life or specific states of mind (as in the case of the consultation of the skeptical Three Kings, in the scene of the *Adoration of Jesus* in the right panel opposite the entrance).

At the bottom right, there is a slightly hidden tomb of a member of the *Baronceli* family dated around 1327. It is pinnacled, with spiral columns, and has been attributed to Giovanni di Balduccio, one of Tino da Camaino's assistants.

The scenes adorning the chapel depict (starting from the top left) *Saint Joachim Banished from the Temple, the Annunciation* and others in the evangelistic tradition. But certainly, the most outstanding of all these frescoes is the *Wedding of the Virgin* (the last one on the right on the left wall) in which Taddeo Gaddi seems to acquire his own, autonomous artistic dimension with respect to Giotto's, giving the figures more brio and suppleness. However, we must also note how the artist, who was celebrated by his contemporaries for his care and skill in depicting architecture, almost like a new Vitruvius or Dinocratus (two architects from antiquity) in the scenes of the *Joachim Banished from the Temple,* and the *Presentation of the Virgin,* depicted a great basilica in two different views from below.

On the back wall, opposite the entrance is the fine *Annunciation to the*

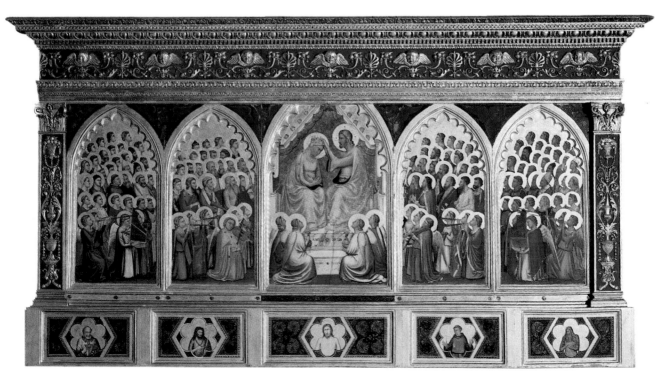

Page 38: *Scenes from the Life of the Virgin, on the walls of the chapel,* by Taddeo Gaddi; page 39: *Annunciation to the Shepherds,* by Taddeo Gaddi.

Shepherds, with an excellent nocturnal rendering of the scene, illuminated by the glow of artificial light, while on the right wall of the chapel is the fifteenth century *Madonna of the Girdle*, a fresco considered a typical example of how Bastiano Mainardi received a series of artistic stimuli in line with the most modern tendencies of Ghirlandaio's School (with the large landscape and sky with angels that recall those by Verrocchio).

In the chapel there is also a large polyptych portraying the *Coronation of the Virgin*, with several figured doors and gold decorations signed by Giotto; it is believed to be one of his last works. It was painted with much participation on the part of the artists from Giotto's workshop, and specifically Taddeo Gaddi, especially in the lateral images, even if the signature is Giotto's *"opus Magistri Jocit"* (the frame dates from the XV century).

● *Sacristy*

DOOR TO THE CORRIDOR OF THE NOVITIATE

We reach the corridor that leads to the Sacristy and then to the Medici Chapel known as "of the Novitiate", through a door built by Michelozzo di Bartolommeo, architect to Cosimo de'Medici in the fifteenth century. It is an opening with fine quality pietra serena decorations. But most of all, it is in keeping with the trend of recovering ancient models, so that some have likened it to a tabernacle like the ones in the church of Orsanmichele (with similarities, in particular, to the aedicula of *St. Louis*). In fact, for the door of Santa Croce, it is a structure consisting of two pillars placed like door jambs to outline the entrance. They are fluted and characterized with a Corinthian capital, above which is a figured band with heads of putti and garlands (frieze) topped by a triangular fronton. The novelty was in the fact that it was not sloping, like similar Gothic tops, but based on ancient Roman reliefs and ruins. The XV century carved and inlaid door leaves were made by Giovanni di Michele.

Corridor leading to the Sacristy and the Chapel of the Novitiate.

ACCESS CORRIDOR TO THE SACRISTY AND THE CHAPEL OF THE NOVITIATE

The corridor is characterized by three large windows with round-headed arches, that were divided by Michelozzo into three smaller openings (triple-lighted windows). And although they are in line with Medieval tradition as regards the openings, they were highly innovative in the light of the new humanistic trends because they were no longer topped by pointed arches, rather round ones, and mainly the median columns are carved with the usual attention for the recovery of the classical style and are rounded at the top.

The entire corridor is of great architectural interest, because it is topped by a long barrel vault. This was much in vogue in mid-fifteenth century Florence instead of the more traditional Medieval cross vault. Thus this type of vault - not withstanding the many construction difficulties it created - was used in a whole series of works for which Leon Battista Alberti's advice was accepted by the critics, in view of a close reproposal of classic models.

The Sacristy;
below, from the left: ***wooden inlay with a vase of flowers*** (detail of one of the doors on the cabinet),
wooden cabinet (detail of the panels).

Illuminated Manuscripts;
below: *reliquary containing*
St. Francis of Assisi's habit
(XVIII cent.).

On the right wall, immediately after the entrance door, there is a painting of The *Deposition of Christ* that was originally in the **sixth room** of the Museo dell'Opera. It was painted by Alessandro Allori (1535-1607), a pupil of Bronzino who was active during the second half of the sixteenth century, with a great sense of the monumental that was most certainly of Michelangesque inspiration.

We enter the *Sacristy* via a wooden door, on the left, with panels that are carved in the center and inlaid along the edges, that has been attributed to Filippo Brunelleschi.

The Sacristy is a large square room with a trussed wooden ceiling built by the Peruzzi family around 1340. On the right wall there is a series of frescoes, including the *Ascent to the Calvary* attributed to Spinello Aretino; in the center a *Crucifixion* by Taddeo Gaddi, and on the right, the *Resurrection* by Niccolò Gerini; the *Ascension*, higher up on the wall has been attributed to one of Gerini's pupils (or even to Gerini). These frescoes are more traditional in style when compared to the innovative ones in the adjacent Rinuccini Chapel. Against the lower part of the wall, as in the center of the room, there is a series of fifteenth century cabinets with reliquaries (there is a piece of St. Francis' habit), choir-books and antiphonaries dating from between the fourteenth and seventeenth centuries. The doors and many parts of these cabinets were carved and inlaid by Giovanni di Michele, at the beginning of the six-

teenth century by Nanni Unghero, while part of the corner bench on the left, on the Rinuccini Chapel side dates from the early fourteenth century and probably was part of a larger cabinet from which the surviving panels, attributed to Taddeo Gaddi are now in the Gallery of the Accademia.

On the left wall there is a bust of *Christ,* in glazed polychrome terracotta made by Giovanni della Robbia at the beginning of the sixteenth century and a lavabo with wooden doors dating from the XV century. The furnishings were masterfully made by Pagno di Lapo Portigiani (1408-1470) who, working with Michelozzo along with a whole series of other artisans generally defined as "Brunelleschian" or "minor", with his refined crafting skills succeeded in spreading the new Tuscan Humanistic style mainly in Bologna.

All the remaining walls of the *Sacristy* are decorated with frescoed panels in different colors that are supposed to resemble fine marble paneling. It was probably a fifteenth century wall treatment in line with the Medici renewals.

THE RINUCCINI CHAPEL

This chapel opens onto the Sacristy, facing the main door, as a sort of annex (rectangular apse), and was built by the Guidotti family. The chapel is reached via a Gothic gate from 1371, passing under an arch, which like the rest of the walls and vault is decorated with an important cycle of frescoes (1365, circa) by Giovanni da Milano and a master from Orcagna's school, who still unknown, is generally called the "Master of the Rinuccini Chapel". On the right wall of the chapel are the *Scenes from the Life of Mary Magdalen* all by Giovanni da Milano (except for the last two).

Starting from the top: *The Magdalen Washing the Feet of Christ; The Saint Praying to Him; The Resurrection of Lazarus;, the scene of Noli me tangere; The Magdalen Witnessing a Miracle* (these last two panels are by the "Master of the Chapel").

The Rinuccini Chapel with the Gothic (or neo-Gothic gate).

Presentation of the Virgin in the Temple, and *Wedding of the Virgin*, by the "Master of the Rinuccini Chapel";
below: ***The Birth of Mary and The Angel Meeting St. Ann,*** (details), by Giovanni da Milano.

On the left wall are *Scenes from the Life of the Virgin*, a favorite theme for artists of Giotto's school. These, however, were painted by Giovanni da Milano, an artist from Lombardy who worked in Florence between 1346 and 1369. He distinguished himself from his contemporaries by his northern training, which however was not lacking in strong Sienese influence, with a marked development of naturalistic elements and concrete situations combined with a solemn rituality in the characters' gestures. He also used brilliant colors from red to yellow which were balanced by the pink flesh tones that aimed at giving the figures a precise sense of vitality. In this cycle Giovanni da Milano's originality is expressed mainly in the marked desire to place the scenes in a familiar setting, and for the total lack of Gothic drama in the gestures, and by the solemnity and slow rhythm with which he infused the delicate female figures. The Milanese painter did not finish his work on either of the chapel walls, and it was picked up by the "Master of the Rinuccini Chapel" or perhaps by Giovanni Gaddi, another talented painter.

On the wall, starting from the top, there is *"St. Joachim Banished from the Temple"* in which we can see extreme attention to architectural details with a five-nave basilica with semi-circular rather than pointed arches as were used during the Gothic era. Then there is *The Angel Meeting St. Ann; The Birth of Mary*, where the simplicity of the frescoed room is offset by the elegant robes of the handmaids. Next is the *Presentation in the Temple*; the *Wedding* (these last two were done by the Master of the Chapel who tried to adapt to the Milanese painter's style).

On the vault are the Redeemer and the Four Prophets, and on the altar a polyptych by Giovanni del Biondo, dated 1379 with a typically Gothic frame: in the center is the Virgin Enthroned with the Child, while the panel immediately below (the predella) portrays the Adoration of the Magi.

MONASTERY WING KNOWN AS THE NOVITIATE

Where the Leather School is today, there was once an interesting wing of the monastery built or expanded in the fifteenth century by Michelozzo according to Vasari, under Medici patronage as we can see from the family's coat of arms on the ceilings of several rooms. In the **first room** in the lunette above the second door there is a fresco of *St. Francis Blessing the Novices*, from Ghirlandaio's school, late fifteenth century; beyond that door, there is a long corridor with a barrel vault, like the most typical Albertian structures that leads to the rooms that were originally the monks' cells, each with a barrel vault but at a 90° angle with respect to the ceiling of the central corridor. At the end of the corridor there is a lunette with an *Annunciation*, again from Ghirlandaio's school.

Top: *Procession of the Magi and Adoration of the Shepherds* central detail of the predella polyptych by Giovanni del Biondo; above: *Virgin Enthroned with the Child,* detail of the polyptych by Giovanni del Biondo; opposite: *Annunciation,* from Ghirlandaio's school.

Chapel of the Novitiate;
below: *Virgin and Child
with Saints* (detail of the
polyptych on the right wall).

CHAPEL OF THE NOVITIATE *or of Piero dei Medici*

Returning to the corridor that starts from the transept of the basilica, at the end, on the left is the Chapel of the Novitiate, a room that was created as a place for private prayer for Cosimo and mainly his son, Piero dei Medici in 1445. In the XVI century Giorgio Vasari described the chapel as having been designed by Michelozzo di Bartolomeo alone in the monastery of Santa Croce. It is a rectangular room with a small room that was added on the side facing the entrance, on the basis of the same typology used by Filippo Brunelleschi in the Old Sacristy of San Lorenzo. The ceiling consists of two cross ribs which rest on Ionic corbels (capitals against the wall) probably motivated by the fact that the high walls of the chapel, that soar on the outside with respect to the wings of the monastery could not have supported a barrel vault that was so much in fashion at the time.

In the chapel, on the altar there is a glazed terra-cotta altar piece by Andrea della Robbia (circa 1480, the era of Lorenzo the Magnificent), over which there is a stained glass window by Alessio Baldovinetti, who also worked with Antonio Rossellino after 1460 on the Albertian Chapel of the Cardinal of Portugal in San Miniato al Monte. On the right wall is a *Monument to Francesco Lombardi* consisting of fifteenth century fragments including a *Virgin and Child* from the School of Donatello.

Leaving the chapel and returning to the Basilica, on the left is the *Monument*

Glazed terra-cotta altarpiece by Andrea della Robbia.
below: *Apparition of the Bull on the Gargano* (detail) by the "Master of the Velluti Chapel".

to Lorenzo Bartolini, by Pasquale Romanelli, who made it in memory of his teacher around 1850. Bartolini (1777-1850) was one of the greatest Florentine artists of his time, and notwithstanding his aloof and bad-tempered character, was certainly one of the initiators of that separation from the Neoclassic style then in vogue, in the name of a Purism founded on a careful study of Florentine Renaissance sculpture.

● *Chapels at the end of the transept*

VELLUTI CHAPEL *or San Michele Chapel*

This contains frescoes in very poor condition by a pupil of Cimabue known as the "Master of the Velluti Chapel". On the right wall is the *Victory of the Archangel Michael*, and on the left wall the *Apparition of the Bull on the Gargano*, where the Archangel had a church built. On the altar there is a fourteenth century polyptych by Giovanni del Biondo with a fifteenth century predella by Neri di Bicci.

Above, from the left: *the vault* with frescoes by Giovanni da San Giovanni, *Discovery of the Cross,* by Giovanni Bilivert; below: *two angels with a scroll,* detail of the Ecstasy of St. Francis, by Matteo Rosselli.

CALDERINI CHAPEL *or Riccardi*

This chapel, which also belonged to the Riccardi family was refurnished at the beginning of the XVII century by the architect Gherardo Silvani (1620 circa) with the help of a group of painters including the great names in seventeenth century Florence. They included Giovanni Mannozzi, known as Giovanni da San Giovanni who brought the fresco technique back into fashion by modernizing it with very fluid, diluted colors and with vast fields of color. In fact, Giovanni da San Giovanni did the frescoes on the vault and lunettes, which, like the rest of his art tend to seek an immediacy of the tale with even "common" colors.

On the right wall there is a canvas painting of the *Ecstasy of St. Francis* by Matteo Rosselli, the artist in whose workshop Giovanni da San Giovanni was trained, and who, along with Giovanni Bilivert is considered one of the initiators of that style known as "flamboyant melodrama" because of the ample participation of the figures in the episodes.

On the left wall, the painting of *St. Lawrence Giving Alms* is by Domenico Passignano, a Venetian artist who contributed to the development of the devotional register of XVII century Florentine painting with rich sacred representations.

The *Discovery of the Cross* on the altar is by Bilivert.

The Giugni Chapel.

GIUGNI CHAPEL *or Bonaparte*

Inside this chapel is the *Tomb of Julie Clary Bonaparte* (on the right) dated 1845, by Luigi Pampaloni who, notwithstanding the fact that the current sensitivity no longer liked typical neoclassical style monuments, did not renounce the use of the sarcophagus to hold the remains of the deceased. This sarcophagus was decorated on the basis of neo-fifteenth century tastes, making it a fine example of the passage and mediation between two different moments in the city's artistic choices.

In the chapel there is also the *Monument to Charlotte Bonaparte*, (on the left) by Lorenzo Bartolini (1839), like his first work inside the basilica. Neither did Bartolini renounce the use of an urn, but the comparison with the nearby *Monument to Julie Clary Bonaparte* shows how the sculptor was much more attentive, not so much to reproposing classical models, but to the rendering of those models in Renaissance-style versions.

PERUZZI CHAPEL

Along with the nearby Bardi Chapel this is one of the two surviving chapels by Giotto in Santa Croce, as opposed to the four that are mentioned by early sources.

The Peruzzi Chapel was built a few years before the Bardi chapel, on commission from the wealthy banking family. It has an important cycle of frescoes by Giotto during his mature period, that is, after the Assisi and Padua experiences. The scenes, covered with whitewash in the eighteenth century and then "rediscovered" in 1852 were in-painted where parts were missing (arches, landscapes that had considerably depressed the Giottesque atmosphere of the composition). Then, after most of the nineteenth century in-painting was removed, towards the end of the nineteen sixties they were treated with the "map method", highlighting the original parts and eliminating the later additions, thus preferring to highlight the gaps over the visual unity thereby rendering some parts indeed difficult to read.

The value of these *Scenes from the Lives of Saint John the Baptist and Saint John the Evangelist,* datable around 1317-1318, is considerable in the context of the development of Medieval art. Giotto made great innovations in the pictorial language of the era, aiming at the expression of a strong sense of monumentality in his portrayals through the mass arrangement of the figures, the painting of architecture, without however, neglecting the most recent conquests of contemporary Florentine Gothic painting. In particular, the high

level of Giotto's composition is expressed on the right wall dedicated to St. John the Evangelist, in the portrayal of the *Saint in Patmos* (above), where the painter aimed at a highly effective fusion of the sky and sea. It recalls the pictoricism and attention to transitions mediated between the colors that was one of the most innovative of Giotto's conquests presented in the Scrovegni Chapel in Padua. Then comes the *Saint Resuscitating Druisianai*, with the large absidial tribune of a Medieval basilica in the background, that still fills the scene, and the peculiar rendering of the participation in the event painted on the faces of the onlookers. Then comes the *Ascension of the Saint into Heaven* where the setting is decidedly defined by the surrounding architecture.

These last two compositions follow the scheme of the emphasis that Giotto placed on a very special moment of the story by having the main action take place in the center, on the basis of the new development of the master's language that is seeking marked architectural monumentality in the scenes.

On the left wall of the chapel are the *Scenes from the Life of Saint John the Baptist*, with, from the top, S*t. Zacharias Receiving the Annunciation of the Birth of St. John*, followed by the *Birth of St. John the Baptist*, and then *Herod's Banquet*, a scene in which Giotto's embryonic research on perspective touches one of the peaks of pre-humanistic experimentation in the large, obviously three-dimensional pavilion and mainly in the three-quarter view (a theme that was to become dear to the followers of Giotto's school in Santa Croce, and specifically Taddeo Gaddi in the Baroncelli Chapel).

Above: *Herod's Banquet,* by Giotto; opposite page: *Herod's Banquet* (detail), by Giotto.

BARDI CHAPEL

Painted by Giotto after 1317 (probably around 1325) and hence in the last phase of his artistic maturity, this cycle with *Scenes from the Life of St. Francis*, picks up a theme that the painter had already treated in his great fresco cycle in Assisi in the last few years of the thirteenth century. Even these frescoes, that were done "dry" and are better preserved than those in the Peruzzi Chapel, were whitewashed in the XVIII century to be rediscovered in 1852 and restored and in-painted by Gaetano Bianchi. In the sixties, they too, were liberated from the nineteenth century in-painting, thereby revealing the missing parts of the composition. The chronological sequence of the events in the life of St. Francis is portrayed in these scenes, starting from the left wall to the right wall, with a rhythm that is more official as compared to the marked search for humanity in the figures that characterized the analogous cycle in Assisi.

In the upper left, *St. Francis Gives Away His Belongings* with once again an image of three quarters of the large central building, marked by an already highly classicist style (so much so that in his fifteenth century relief sculpture of the *Miracle of the Repentant Son* for the altar of the Saint, Donatello would use the typology portrayed here by Giotto). Next is the scene of the *Saint Appearing Before St. Anthony of Padua Preaching at Arles*. In this picture we must note the sense of astonishment that Giotto painted on the faces of the onlookers, as well as the sense of devotion and majesty conveyed by the figure of St. Francis. Both of these scenes are similar to those in Assisi as regards subject and arrangement, but in Santa Croce the new sense of space that animates

The Death of the Saint;
below: *Visions of Brother Augustine and Bishop Guido of Assisi* (detail), two works by Giotto.

60

Preceding page: *Apparition of St. Francis* (detail) by Giotto. Above: *Trial* by Fire Before the Sultan; below: *Saint Claire,* works by Giotto.

Giotto's later art makes a strong impression, up to the portrayal of the children in the first one who, though held back by their mothers try to throw stones at the Saint. Giotto's language is once against renewed in the systematic search of the different renderings in the treatment of light and colors within the whole composition, with great attention to shadows and chiaroscuro effects. The last fresco on this wall is the *Jerome Looking for the Stigmata*. In this image we can see the extreme delicacy that Giotto used in the faces and heads of St. Francis' followers, while the Giottesque innovation in the depiction of the characters' expressions, moods and humanity (features that had already been the great explosive novelty in the Assisi cycle) is still lively.

On the right wall, are the *Approval of the Rule* (top) and the *Trial by Fire Before the Sultan* (middle) where the chromatic accent is important in the contrasts, as, for example in the figure of the black servant dressed in white robes and turban. And finally there is the scene of the *Visions of Brother Augustine and Bishop Guido of Assisi*, in which the composure seems to predominate as the highest achievement of Giotto's narrative.

The panel on the altar with *The Life of St. Francis* dates from the thirteenth century.

61

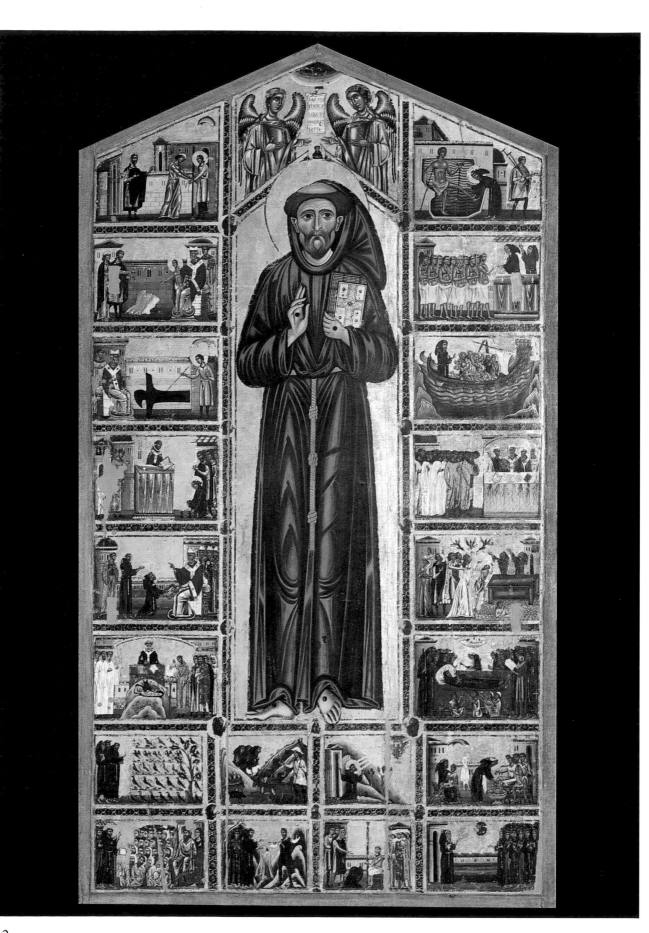

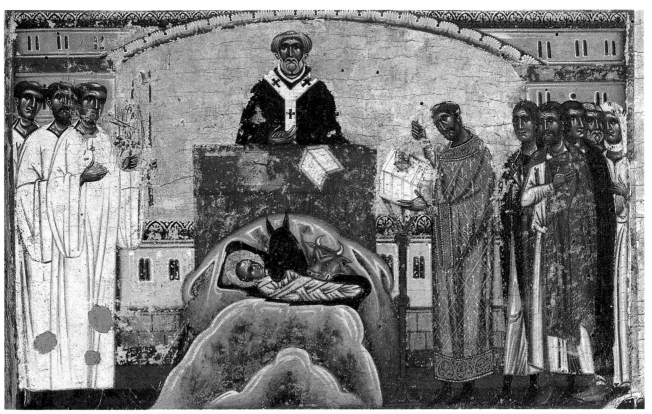

Preceding page: on the altar, *panel with Scenes from the Life of St. Francis,* by Barone Berlinghieri. Above: *The Manger and the Church;* below: *St. Francis Preaching to the Birds.*

Preceding page: *the Main Chapel.*
Above: *Heraclius Enters Jerusalem with the Cross,* by Agnolo Gaddi;
below: *detail.*

THE MAIN CHAPEL

The Main Chapel (formerly the Alberti chapel) which is now the choir of the basilica was commissioned by Jacopo degli Alberti. It has a polygonal plan, with an umbrella ribbed vault and three large double-lighted windows on the walls. It seems to derive from Transalpine Gothic architecture rather than belong to Italian, and specifically Florentine building tradition. The frescoes and the stained glass windows were done by Agnolo Gaddi (Taddeo's son), with the help of artists from his workshop. Around 1380 he painted the cycle of the *Legend of the Cross,* according to the "Golden Legend" by Iacopo da Varagine, a very famous Medieval text that Piero della Francesca used for his frescoes in Arezzo during the fifteenth century.

The story, told in a series of scenes of brief episodes enlivened by the typical late fourteenth century clothing lacks the monumentality and careful measurement of space of Giotto's style. It begins at the upper right with *St. Michael Giving Seth a Branch from the Tree of Knowledge*; it is followed by sections with the *Planting of the Branch on Adam's Tomb*; the *Growth of the Tree* and the *Construction of a Bridge from its Wood, The Queen of Sheba Kneels Before It and Solomon Then Sinks the Beam*; the I*sraelites Find the Beam and Make the Cross for Christ*; *St. Helena Finds the Cross.*
On the left wall: *St. Helena Brings the Cross Back to Jerusalem*; the *King of*

Persia Steals the Cross; *The Dream of the Victorious Byzantine Emperor Heraclius*; and *After Having Beheaded the King of Persia Heraclius Enters Jerusalem with the Cross*.

This is the dissolution of the Giottoesque world and its principles in a fairytale atmosphere that reproposes nothing, especially in its refigurations of greater figurative fatigue, of the Master's last conquests and reflections in the Peruzzi and Bardi chapels. However, these frescoes are not lacking in rich details, or marked attention to the types depicted that are reproposed in a standardized manner at the cartoon level without forgetting an albeit limited quest for depth in the individual scenes.

The polyptych on the altar (it was redone during the XIX century) portrays the *Virgin, Saints and the Fathers of the Church* by various late XIV century artists, while the large Crucifix above it is by the "Maestro di Figline", who worked in Gottio's workshop, and in the fourteenth century used the model proposed by Cimabue in 1280.

Above: *the Israelites Find the Beam and Make the Cross for Christ,* by Agnolo Gaddi; below: *St. Helena Finds the Cross,* (detail).

Above: *Polyptych,* on the altar;
opposite: *St. Helena Finds
the Cross,* (detail).

TOLOSINI CHAPEL *or Spinelli*

Outside and above the chapel (that had belonged to the Spinelli and then Sloane families) there is a section of fresco (largely repainted) by the Maestro di Figline who is also believed to have made the stained glass window. According to some sources, Giotto frescoed the interior of this chapel which is now decorated with paintings done by Gasparo Martellini in 1837. The two paintings are *The Vow of the Florentines After the Plague of 1633* on the right, and the *Dogma of the Immaculate Conception* on the left.

BENCI CHAPEL *or Capponi*

This chapel (dedicated to St. Ann, and later property of the Capponi family) was transformed into a memorial chapel for the dead of World War I in 1926. It was designed by the architect Enrico Lusini and dedicated to the Madre Italiana. Inside is the statue of the Pietà by Libero Andreotti, sculpted with great composure and linearity. Andreotti was given the commission after having completed two parts of a competition. The judging panel included Armando Brasini, Gustavo Giovannoni and Ugo Ojetti, who rejected Raffaello Fagnoni's idea of placing the statue in the crypt beneath the main altar, gave Andreotti the first prize for the "original clarity of deisgn and composition. The reliefs on the sides of the chapel are by the same artist.

RICASOLI CHAPEL

This chapel, dedicated to St. Anthony of Padua was completely remodeled in 1836. There are paintings of the *Miracles of St. Anthony* by Luigi Sabatelli and his sons, Francesco and Giuseppe.

BARDI DI LIBERTÀ CHAPEL *or Pulci - Beraldi*

The chapel is decorated with a series of frescoes by Bernardo Daddi and his helpers, dated around 1330. Daddi, who had been one of Giotto's helpers for nearly twenty years, frescoed the chapel while his master was still alive, and it is likely that Giotto gave him some advice as well.

On the right wall: the *Martyrdom of St. Lawrence* clearly shows how the marked sophistication in chromatic variations achieved by Giotto in his last works became the artistic goal to which Bernardo Daddi aspired. However, while probing the possibilities of chiaroscuro and shadow in a rather experimental manner, Daddi did not create scenes of great luminous clarity. The gestures of the figures intent on martyring the saint are extremely interesting, they are extremely dynamic and contrast strongly with the nearly wooden stiffness of St. Lawrence.

On the left wall: The *Condemnation and Martyrdom of St. Stephen* in which the most strictly Florentine line of Giottoism reveals its most peculiar features. Before turning towards the conquests of contemporary Sienese painting, Daddi created figurations of great balance without extreme surges, but with marked attention and accuracy. These characters know how to mediate between the need for a rather harsh narrative and attention to feeling. The glazed terracotta *Madonna and Child Enthroned with Saint John the Evangelist*, altarpiece was made by Giovanni della Robbia at the end of the XV century.

Above: *the Martyrdom of St. Lawrence* (detail), by Bernardo Daddi; opposite: *Virgin Enthroned with the Child and St. John the Evangelist,* glazed terra-cotta altarpiece by Giovanni della Robbia.

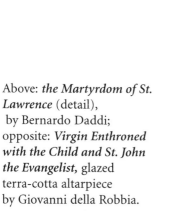

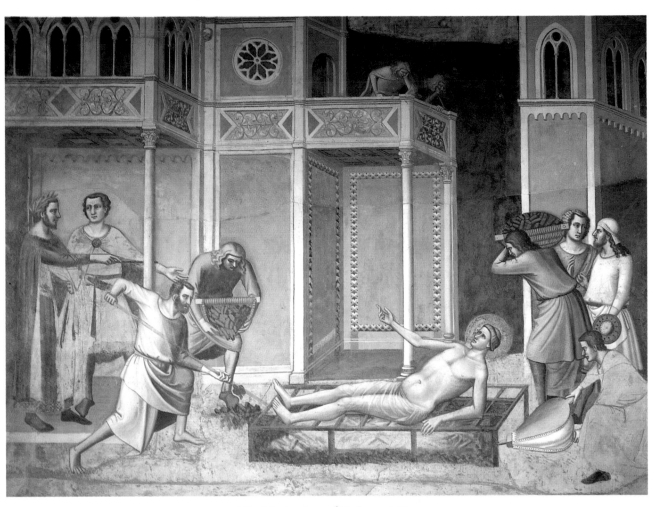

The Martyrdom of St. Lawrence,
below: *Condemnation and Martyrdom of St. Stephen,* two works by Bernardo Daddi.

Deposition, from the school
of Taddeo Gaddi.

BARDI CHAPEL *or Chapel of St. Silvester*
(in restoration since 1996)

Frescoed by Maso di Banco around 1340 with scenes from the Iacopo da Varagine's "Golden Legend", the narration focuses on episodes in the life of St. Silvester to whom the entire cycle is dedicated. Maso, together with Taddeo Gaddi and Bernardo Daddi, was among the most outstanding artists in this phase of Florentine painting. But as opposed to the other two, the lessons of Giotto whom he had followed even to Naples remain more present in his compositions, especially in the nearly rigid use of symmetry, as the

*Miracle of the Saint who
Closes the Dragon's Jaws
and Revives Two Wizards,*
by Maso di Banco;
below: *detail.*

Master desired. But it was even the extreme limpidity of the colors that the spreadings offer to the slightly shaded scenes, for the treatment of human or architectural masses with the same logic of rigid blocks (a stereometric logic) that create the visual interchange between architecture and painting that made Maso a true continuer of the line inaugurated by Giotto in Santa Croce. On the left wall, *The Dream of Constantine* (not very visible) has been attributed to one of Maso's helpers. Against the wall, at the bottom are two Gothic tombs: in the niche of the first supported by spiral columns and a Gothic aedicula, there is a fresco of the *Last Judgement and Bettino de' Bardi Kneeling*, which has also been attributed to Maso. In the niche of the second one the fresco of the *Deposition and Doner* was probably painted by Taddeo Gaddi.
On the right wall: *St. Silvester Baptizing the Emperor Constantine*, followed by the *Miracle of the Bull Revived by the Saint*; and the *Miracle of the Saint who Closes the Dragon's Jaws and Revives Two Wizards*. The background of this painting is the Roman Forum, scattered with ruins. It is not only a direct continuation of Giotto's sensitivity - with much attention to the ancient buildings, the reproposal of many decorative structures derived form the ruins or their reutilization - but it is also characterized by the contemporary compenetration between the plastic of the masses and the chromatic and tonal study of the figures that are also treated with a typically architectural eye. In the foreground on the left, in particular, there is an isolated column, its cylindrical shape is precisely matched with the cylindrical volumes of the Saint, the Emperor and the tower on the circle of walls in the background, according to a precise play of compositional counterweights.
The triptych on the altar dates from the fourteenth century.

*The vault of the
Niccolini Chapel.*
Opposite page: *view of
the chapel.*

NICCOLINI CHAPEL

This chapel that is reached via a door closed off by a seventeenth century gate, comprising two Corinthian columns supporting a broken-arch fronton, stands at the extreme right of the end of the transept. It is rectangular and topped by an interesting seventeenth century (1664) elliptical dome. It was built by Giovan Antonio Dosio between 1575 and 1584 in a style that considered the architectural order as the basis for structuring space. Therefore, it is a tight grid created by the rhythm of the pilaster strips that are arranged to frame the interior surfaces, inside which all the decorative apparatus were placed. These include the rich marble inlays on the walls, one of the first examples of such usage; or the fine paintings by Alessandro Allori (the *Assumption* and the *Coronation of the Virgin*) and the rich frescoes by Volterrano in the cupola; the sculptures by Pietro Francavilla, a pupil of Giambologna (on the Niccolini tomb, with *Aaron* on the right, and *Moses* on the left, and statues of *St. Agnes*, *Prudence* and *Charity* in the niches). In brief, it is adorned according to a concept of architecture and all the arts in a Counter Reformation key, notwithstanding the lavishness of the decorations, in light of a new rigor that was foreign to the eccentricities and oddities of which Bernardo Buontalenti was one of the maximum exponents in late sixteenth century Florence.

BARDI CHAPEL *(di Vernio)*

The chapel is closed off by a large iron gate made in 1335 and a XIV century tomb of the Bardi family with an interesting multifoiled arch. The wooden *Crucifix* on the altar was carved by Donatello around 1425, and Filippo Brunelleschi had criticized it as being too realistic. Vasari recounts an interesting anecdote. "Donato [Donatello] made a wooden crucifix over which he took extraordinary pains. When he had finished it, convinced that he had produced a very rare work, he asked his close friend, Filippo Brunelleschi, for his opinion. But Filippo, in view of what he had already been told by Donatello was expecting to be shown something far better; and when he saw what it was he merely smiled to himself. At this Donatello begged him for the sake of their friendship to say what he thought of it. So Filippo, being always read to oblige answered that it seemed to him that Donatello had put on the cross the body of a peasant, not the body of Jesus Christ which was most delicate and in every part the most perfect human form ever created."[1] This feature of Donatello's work, the marked realism was praised or denigrated by the critics over the centuries, so that the *Crucifix* in any event became one of the high points of Florentine Humanistic artistic production.

In the chapel there is also a gilded ciborium, a true wooden architectural machine built according to the model of a central-plan temple by Giorgio Vasari, and two sixteenth century angels that Vasari made for the main altar of the Basilica which was later taken down.

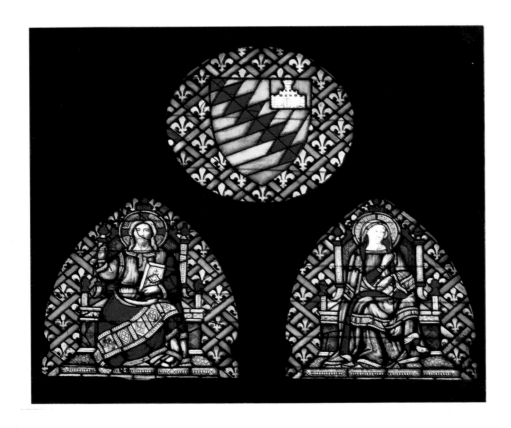

Preceding page: *wooden Crucifix,* by Donatello. Opposite: *stained glass window* (late XIV century).

Tomb of Sofia Zamoyska,
by Lorenzo Bartolini.

SALVIATI CHAPEL *or Chapel of San Lorenzo*

The Chapel of St. Lawrence (also known as the Machiavelli Chapel) was redesigned by the architect Gherardo Silvani in 1611. Inside (restorations began in 1996) there are many plaques including one on the floor dedicated to the philosopher Giovanni Gentile who was killed in 1945, the *Tomb of Sofia Zamoyska* (in the middle on the left) from 1837-44 is one of the finest works from Lorenzo Bartolini's last years. Once again, the tomb is based on fifteenth century models, with the deceased laying on a bed, with a tondo with a *Madonna* above, it, based on those made by Rossellini. The deceased's face, however is very natural, like the folds of the cover (so much so that it aroused the client's criticism who feared that visitors would note signs of her dying agony).

The altar with the *Martyrdom of St. Lawrence* was done by the Veronese painter, Jacopo Ligozzi at the end of the XVI century. In this painting we can still see Michelangelesque compositional modules, while the artist also dedicated great care to warm, rich colors, typical of the new season of Florentine painting. And in Ligozzi's case it was even more marked because of his Veneto background.

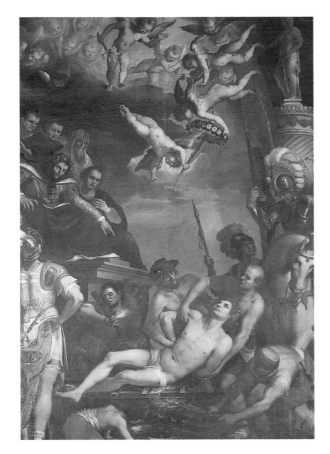

From the left: *Martyrdom of St. Lawrence,* altarpiece by Jacopo Lignozzi; *Monument to Raffaello Morghen* by Odoardo Fantacchiotti.

● *Left nave*

(starting from the back near the transept)

This was part of the old church, of which parts can still be seen by going down the staircase.

MONUMENT TO RAFFAELLO MORGHEN

This monument, dedicated to the famous sculptor was done by Odoardo Fantacchiotti in 1854 on the basis of a sketch made ten years earlier. It is typical of Tuscan Purism, which reproposed the most emblematic styles of Florentine history and culture, and specifically the golden era between the fifteenth and sixteenth centuries.

MONUMENT TO LEON BATTISTA ALBERTI

Built along the central nave, the monument was made by the sculptor Lorenzo Bartolini to honor the great Florentine humanist whose remains were lost shortly after his death in 1472. Bartolini's sculpture, is based on a triangle and resolves with a great plastic projection; it portrays Alberti in the center, with a nude torso flanked by two allegorical figures of young men, also covered by simple drapings that are quite unusual for a monument inside a church. The rather showy movement the sculptor impressed in the poses of the figures has a precise counterpart in coordinated compositional lines, like the legs that are forward, or the torch raised high by the youth on the right which balances Alberti's outstretched arm (held by the seated youth).

SIXTH ALTAR

This altar contains the fine *Pentecost* that Giorgio Vasari painted in 1568, portraying the Virgin and Apostles at prayer. The human landscape in the painting is quite articulated and characterized by the intersection of circular compositional rhythms (with the characters that practically encircle the Virgin), combined with a triangular pattern emphasized by the direction of the rays of the descending Holy Spirit, which stand out like luminous flashes against the background.

MONUMENT TO CARLO MARSUPPINI

This monument, honoring Carlo Marsuppini (1398-1453) was carved by Desiderio da Settignano shortly after 1453. Marsuppini had succeeded Leonardo Bruni as Secretary of the Florentine Republic, and was preceptor to Piero de'Medici and Lorenzo the Magnificent. In this monument the sculptor shows that he had well learned Bernardo Rosselino's lesson, who between 1445-1447 had already built the aedicula wall tomb for Leonardo Bruni in the opposite nave of Santa Croce. According to historiographical sources predating Vasari who attributes the entire work to Desiderio, even Verrocchio may have had a hand in carving this tomb, and in particular the angel holding the garland above and to the right of the lunette. However, these executors of sculptural decorations could not have but made and personalized a design by Leon Battista Alberti who, not only was a close friend of Marsuppini, but who ten years after the monument to Bruni, succeeded in inserting a whole series of details that the critics have rightly linked to the reflection of a scenographic sensitivity. In particular, there is a series of design devices which are typical of Alberti's world, such as the strongly pyramidal rhythm that takes flight upwards, as suggested by the entire base on which the elaborate sarcophagus rests. The base is composed of well-balanced sloping steps. Thus, the sarcophagus itself, with the fine scrolls that frame the lions claws which support it, and the imbricated sarcophagus above, is linked to Roman pieces from the era of Hadrian and then Antonius. The definite Albertian origins of the tomb arrangement can be seen in a series of elements which strongly qualify its appearance: the large, antiquary vase at the top with two large festoons hanging from the handles; the festoons find a close parallel in those of the Tempio Malatestiano in Rimini. Then, there are the capitals of the two pilaster strips that frame the monument, with the double scrolls that are typical of Albertian languages, and finally there is the shell below the sarcophagus with the large plumed wings once again typical of Alberti in using similar emblems and associating various symbolic elements (here the shell is a metaphor of the soul joined to the wings, a specific reference to the fleeting nature of existence). Desiderio da Settignano reached one of the high points of his art in the decoration of the drapings and the face of the deceased.

Detail of the corner pilaster strip.

81

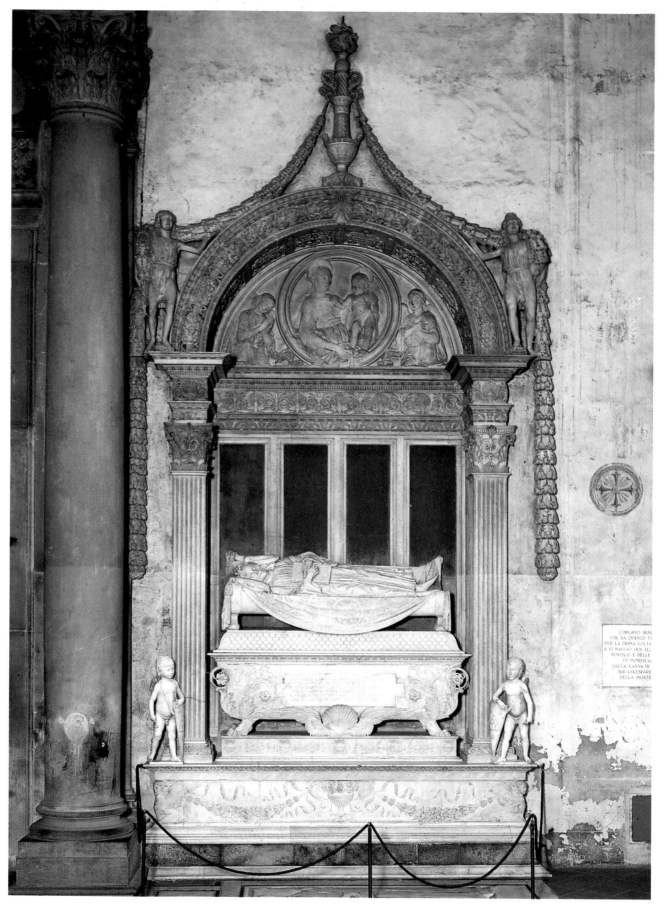

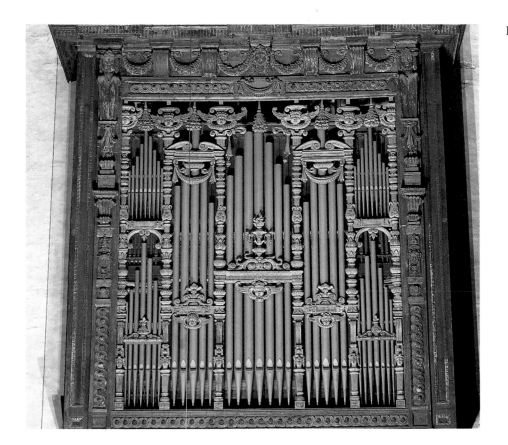

Preceding page: *monument to
Carlo Marsuppini,*
by Desiderio da Settignano.
Opposite: *the organ,*
by Noferi da Cortona.

SECONDARY EXIT DOOR AND NORTHERN LOGGIA

Above the door there is a great monumental organ dating from 1579 by Nofri da Cortona. The fresco of the *Assumption of the Virgin* to the left of the organ has been attributed to Agnolo Gaddi.
The door leads to the external loggia against the left side of the basilica where there is a series of tombs (currently under restoration). Only the *Monument to Francesco Pazzi*; made by a follower of Tino da Camaino in the XIV century remains on the right. The use of the classic female figures (caryatids) supporting the sarcophagus which is carved with three figures inside ratiocinative typically Gothic geometric reliefs (this is the same style that would be seen again a century later in the panels on the door of the baptistry) is very interesting.

FIFTH ALTAR

Returning inside the basilica, the fifth altar has a canvas of the *Ascension* by the Flemish artist Jan van der Straet, one of the master weavers of the Medici tapestry works, known as Stradano. The painting was done in 1569 and the artist did not forget his Northern European training, which is evident in the specific, rendering of a studied sense of color that pervades the entire composition that is wrapped in soft light, and in the great attention to the variations in the different natural states such as the twisted shrubs in the foreground. Once again the general triangular arrangement of the composition with the apex in the head of Christ is mediated and rendered more articulate by the intersection of two semicircular lines, of the which the first above, is represented by the host of angels, and below by the curving lines of the ground beneath the feet of the *Virgin* and the *Apostles*.

PIETÀ

This Pietà on the wall was done by Agnolo di Cosimo known as Il Bronzino, a student of Pontormo and Medici court painter. It is one of the most important paintings placed in the basilica when it was rearranged by Vasari in the sixteenth century. The representation, rich in sparkling tones in the body of Christ which contrasts with the dark background from which the Virgin and putto emerge, succeeds in expressing the intense drama of the action without forgetting a great composure in the rendering of the scene in line with the Counter Reformation sentiments of the Medici court. In this painting we can see the distinctive features of Bronzino's art, for example in the extreme volumes of the figure of Christ.

MONUMENT TO ANGELO TAVANTI

The monument to Tavanti, minister to the Grand Duke Peter Leopold who had summoned the sculptor Ignazio Pellegrini from Rome, was completed in 1773. In the composition the coordinator of the project, the architect Salvetti wanted to use the pyramid type tomb that was enjoying great success at the time in light of the neoclassical fashion. He also added specific references to antique decorations in the sarcophagus with its curved (strigilate) lines, by Francesco and Angelo Giovannozzi, and in the medallion with the portrait of Tavanti which was decorated like a classic cameo by Pellegrini.

FOURTH ALTAR

The Incredulity of St. Thomas by Giorgio Vasari.

THIRD ALTAR

Decorated with the *Supper at Emmaus* by Santi di Tito who, with his chromatic and compositional rigor, definitively renounced the complex style of Florentine Mannerism to approach a more rigorous, Counter Reformation sensibility that led to a recovery of the pacified realism typical of fifteenth century painting. This did not prevent the artist from doing research on the poses of the figures, within a composition of great rigor, and adding notes of movement, especially in the broad gestures of the arms.

Preceding page: *Pietà,*
by Bronzino.
Opposite, top: *The Incredulity
of St. Thomas,*
by Giorgio Vasari;
Supper at Emmaus,
by Santi di Tito.

Resurrection, by Santi di Tito.

SECOND ALTAR

Resurrection by Santi di Tito

TOMB OF GALILEO GALILEI

Designed by Giulio Foggini in 1642 the monument was only completed in the eighteenth century, The *bust* of the famous astronomer and the allegorical portrayal of *Astronomy* (on the left) are by Giovan Battista and Vincenzo Foggini, while the statue of *Geometry* (on the right) was done

GALILAEVS GALILEIVS PATRIC. FLOR.
GEOMETRIAE ASTRONOMIAE PHILOSOPHIAE MAXIMVS RESTITVTOR
NVLLI AETATIS SVAE COMPARANDVS
HIC BENE QVIESCAT
VIX. A. LXXVIII. OBIIT. A. CIƆ. IƆ. C. XXXXI.
CVRANTIBVS AETERNVM PATRIAE DECVS
X. VIRIS PATRICIIS SACRAE HVIVS AEDIS PRAEFECTIS
MONIMENTVM A VINCENTIO VIVIANO MAGISTRI CINERI SIBIQVE SIMVL
TESTAMENTO F.I.
HERES IO. BAPT. CLEMENS NELLIVS IO. BAPT. SENATORIS F.
LVBENTI ANIMO ABSOLVIT.
AN. CIƆ. IƆ. CCXXXVII.

by Gerolamo Ticciati in 1737, the year that the Galileo's remains were finally placed in the tomb. The rhythm of the composition is articulated on a rigid axis of central symmetry highlighted by the bust of the scientist and two curved lines that correspond to the figures on the sides of the sarcophagus.

Two details of the fresco cycle depicting: *The Crucifixion, Ascension, and Jesus' Apparition before the Virgin*, attributed to Mariotto di Nardo; below: *the counterfaçade*.
Opposite page: *Monument to Gino Capponi*, by Antonio Bortone.

CRUCIFIXION, ASCENSION AND JESUS' APPARITION BEFORE THE VIRGIN

These are the remains of a great fresco cycle attributed to Mariotto di Nardo, datable around the beginning of the XV century. There are scant traces of how the basilica's lateral walls looked in the late fourteenth century.

FIRST ALTAR

Here is a *Deposition* by Giovan Battista Naldini which reveals the artist's predilection for the curved lines of the main figures, starting from Mary in the foreground, then continuing to the body of Christ - the key to the entire composition, and then to the crucified thieves in the background.

● *Counterfaçade*

MONUMENT TO GINO CAPPONI

Next to the central door, on the counterfaçade there is the sepulchral monument dedicated to Gino Capponi that was made by the sculpture Antonio Bortone in 1884. The composition combines the neo-fifteenth century wall tomb with the bust of the patriot above, a lovely statue of *Florence* laying a wreath on the tomb (note the border of lilies on the robes, reinforcing the allegory). The finely carved statue gives motion to the whole, with a strong plastic and three-dimensional sense, in line with the development of strictly neo-fifteenth century Tuscan Purism.

MAIN CLOISTER

As we leave the church, on the left we can enter the Main Cloister or First Cloister. Until 1879 it had been divided into two parts by a long wing that was later torn down. On the left side is the fourteenth century portico which currently hosts (in the ground floor rooms) many of the nineteenth century tombstones that had been removed from the old cemetery; above that, below the actual portico there is a collection of coats of arms.

In the back is the Pazzi Chapel, while the former refectory, now the Museo dell'Opera di Santa Croce is on the right. Next come the parts of the monastery that house the existing refectory, Michelozzo's staircase (that connects the rooms with the basilica) and the library that was also designed by Michelozzo.

In the cloister, to the right, beyond the museum wing is a statue of the *Eternal Father*, carved by Baccio Bandinelli in 1549 for the main altar of the cathedral. It is a bit stubby, but where the raised left arm dialogues with the opposite knee raised on the book, it creates a sort of chiasmus that conveys poses of ancient statuary, even if it is erect.

Preceding page: the colossal statue of the *Eternal Father,* by Baccio Bandinelli (1549), and his favorite pupil, Vincenzo de'Rossi,is a perfect synthesis of the various artistic stimuli the artistic acquired during his studies, in harmony with forms derived from Hellenism, the modern statuary of Donatello and Michelangelo, to the works of Andrea del Sarto.
Above: *the Main Cloister;* opposite: *detail of a capital in the Peruzzi Chapel.*

MUSEO DELL'OPERA DI SANTA CROCE

The museum stands in an old part of the monastery that was originally used as the refectory and for other purposes. The exhibition takes up six rooms that contain mostly frescoes dating from the XIV to XVII century which had been removed from the basilica. The museum was opened in 1959 then closed after the 1966 flood that severely damaged many of the artworks in Santa Croce, to be reopened in 1975 (many items are still being restored from the 1966 disaster). Some of the items on display are of great importance in art history.

FIRST ROOM

This is a large, early fourteenth century room that was originally the friars' refectory (hence the long openings in the walls, the large window on the entrance door, and the trussed ceiling). In the lunette above the entrance there is a fragment of Taddeo Gaddi's early fourteenth century *Deposition*. On the right wall there is the large *Crucifix* (done before 1284, but definitely documented in 1288) by Cimabue (1240-1302). Even though Dante mentioned him as the greatest painter before Giotto, we actually know very little about him (he is mentioned as having been in Rome in 1272, and we know of his work in the apse of the Pisa cathedral in 1301-1302). Cimabue, however, has a very important position in Italian painting since his works were the inexorable reference for fourteenth century painters including Giotto himself. Cimabue's definitively attributed works, like those of Nicola Pisano and Arnolfo di Cambio show a clear

Preceding page: frescoes by
Taddeo Gaddi depicting the
Crucifix with the Tree of Life,
and the base, *The Last Supper.*

Byzantine influence. Even though what we know about Cimabue's artistic career is filled with gaps, there is no doubt that the Santa Croce *Crucifix* was once of the high points. Even though it was severely damaged by the 1966 flood, the essential lines, at least have been restored. Today we can still appreciate the composure and mainly the sense of utter abandon revealed by the body of Christ that seems to hang from the nails, a sort of "giant without a spine, abandoned in sublime softness with an abnormally long body that is broader at the hips, in a nearly feminine structure." (Bellosi). We are not certain of exactly where in the basilica this large *Crucifix* was originally placed. We know that it was moved to various places in the church over the centuries as fashions and tastes changed, and that it was even hung beneath the loggia in the First Cloister. Further along in the first room, next to the *Crucifix* there is a detached fresco portraying the *The Friars Minor Arrive in Florence*, by Giovanni del Biondo (1356-1398), a picture of considerable interest for fourteenth century Florentine history. According to the *Fonti Francescane*, two friars came to the city in 1209; having made strict vows of poverty they refused to take alms in the cathedral and thus gave a remarkable example of observance of the Gospels. The fresco is very interesting because it shows one of the earliest images of the Baptistry of San Giovanni and of the Cathedral of Santa Maria del Fiore. On the back wall of the room, there are frescoes by Taddeo Gaddi, *Crucifix with the Tree of Life* (center), and at the base, a *Last Supper*, which have both been largely restored over the centuries, and are very similar to Giotto's style. Once again, the *Tree of Life* is based on a Medieval theological text by St. Bonaventure (portrayed at the foot of the Cross, on the right, pen in hand), entitled *The Wood of Life*, listing the various hierarchies with the figures of the Prophets, the Evangelists, etc. On either side are scenes from the life of *Christ and Saints* (St. Benedict, St. Francis, St. Louis of Toulouse).

On the left wall, after various paintings by Orcagna (note the frgaments of the *Triumph of Death*, and *The Last Judgement* - the second fresco - the scene in which even prelates are judged in the *Inferno*), there is a niche resembling the original tabernacle in the church of Orsanmichele. It contains Donatello's 1442 statue of *St. Louis of Toulouse*, one of the first statues cast in bronze since antiquity. Sometime around 1460 the *St. Louis* was moved to Santa Croce and remained above the main door, on the outside until the façade was rebuilt in the nineteenth century. Vasari considered this statue "bungled and the worst he had ever done", and many critics agreed with this opinion in spite of the fact that Donatello's composition was the fruit of an exceptional idea. The figure of the saint seems to rotate on itself, as if hinged on the pastoral staff in this right hand; it looks like slow motion accentuated by the fold of the cloak toward the left and the extension of a flap to the right. This movement is associated with the strong emphasis of a diagonal axis impressed on the staff, while the saint's face is immersed in a profound, deep ecstasy that contrasts with the dynamism of his body. The top of the staff, is extremely interesting. Donatello designed it similarly to a building with a central plan, like Brunelleschi's lanterns on the dome of Santa Maria del Fiore, or his Rotonda di Santa Maria degli Angeli. In this case, as in most carved or three dimensional architecture built like small models, we cannot exclude the possibility that Donatello received some advice, and perhaps even from Brunelleschi himself.

Near the door leading to the Second Room is the detached fresco from the Cavalcanti chapel, like Donatello's *Annunciation,* and *St. Francis and St. John the Baptist,* by Domenico Veneziano a protegé of Piero dei Medici, Cosimo's son. The fresco is characterized by delicate colors with rich luminous tones, typical of Veneziano's chromatics that never totally neglected his Venetian origins, even in his Florentine works.

St. Francis and St. John the Baptist, by Domenico Veneziano.

Above the door, in a high tondo is *The Prophet David* a fresco attributed to Andrea Orcagna's circles, and in the lunette, the *Coronation of the Virgin* a fine work that the critics had originally attributed to Giotto, but now ascribe to Maso di Bianco (1320-1350).

SECOND ROOM

From the left: detached fresco with the *Virgin and Child Playing*, perhaps by Gherardo Starnina (1350-1413.); on the back wall, *The Dying St. Francis Distributes Bread to the Brothers*, by Jacopo Ligozzi (1547-1626); and fragments of polychrome glass including Saints and Deacons, that can be attributed to an artist very close to Giotto. In the middle of the room are terra-cotta reliefs that had been removed from the top of the aedicula of Donatello's *Cavalcanti Annunciation* after recent restorations.

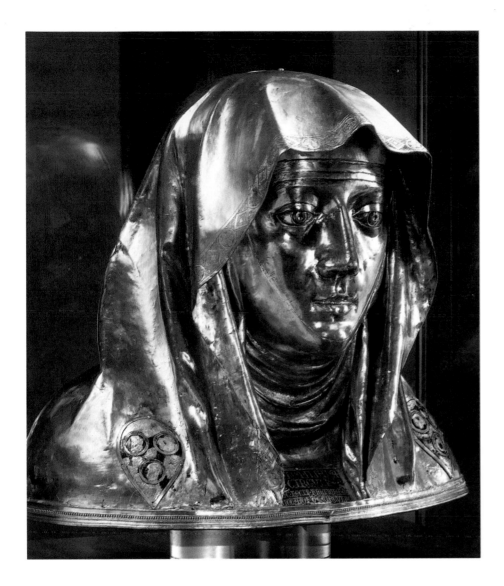

Reliquary-bust of the Blessed Umiliana dei Cerchi, from Orcagna's workshop; below *Bust of the Saint,* black drawing on plaster, attributed to Donatello.

THIRD ROOM

The third room consists of the old Cerchi Chapel, build in the fourteenth century on commission by Frante Arrigo, a relative of the Blessed Umiliana dei Cerchi, renowned Franciscan tertiary in Florence who died in 1246. Today the totally remodeled chapel has a fine *Reliquary-Bust* from 1360 in the middle; it portrays the Blessed Umiliana and was made in Orcagna's workshop. On the walls there is a series of glazed polychrome terra-cottas that were originally altar frontals or predellas, from the Della Robbia workshop.

FOURTH ROOM

There are some very interesting black drawings that have been detached from the plaster, like sinopias, from the Pazzi Chapel. They prove that during a certain period (but we do not know when) there had been an idea of decorating the bare walls of the chapel with frescoes. It has even been hypothesized they were trials by Donatello. These are followed by other detached frescoes datable in the XV century.

Tomb of Gastone della Torre
(detail), Bishop of Aquilieia,
by Tino da Camaino.

FIFTH ROOM

This room contains remains of XIV century marble tombs including the almost intact one (against the back wall) of *Gastone della Torre*, bishop of Aquileia, by Tino da Camaino (1280-1337). In this monument the artist seems quite close to the contemporary Sienese paintings by Ambrogio Lorenzetti, with pictorial accents in full polemic with the plastic and volumetric style of Giovanni Pisano. The white marble tomb, carved shortly after 1318, originally stood in the right nave of the basilica, and then it was moved in the sixteenth century and then again on several occasions. Each of these moves greatly compromised the statue as some parts have been destroyed.

SIXTH ROOM

Here there are series of detached frescoes datable from the XVII and XVIII centuries; the were salvaged during the demolition of the city's old center in the XIX century. They include a portrayal of *Jesus in the Garden and the Magdalen*, and may have been painted by Matteo Reselli around 1615.

Jesus in the Garden and the Magdalen, attributed to Matteo Rosselli.

SECOND CLOISTER OR LARGE CLOISTER

As we leave the museum and go to the right we come to the *Large Cloister* that was completed in 1453, probably by Bernardo Rossellino, on the basis of a traditionalistic architectural language that has round-headed arches over the columns of the lower portico (these arches enhance the formal and design novelty of the trabeated portico in the nearby Pazzi Chapel). The cloister consists of a squared space bounded by a portico with two orders where slim pietra serena columns support the projection of the roof.

To return to the *First Cloister* we go through the big door built in 1450 ca. by Benedetto da Maiano on the basis of strong stylistic similarities with Alberti's language. The Pazzi Chapel is at the rear.

THE PAZZI CHAPEL

It was in 1429 that the Pazzi, one of the richest families in the city and quite feared by the Medici, decided to build this chapel. Between 1430 and 1433 the job was assigned to Filippo Brunelleschi, but upon his death in 1446 not only was work far from completion, but in 1473, the finishes had not been done. This led to the hypothesis that Brunelleschi's models for the chapel were only used to a minimal extent (perhaps only the layout), while the façade and other decorative solutions have recently been attributed to Michelozzo. One more careful interpretation, on the other hand, presumes that Leon Battista Alberti gave advice for the completion of the front that was actually done by artisans under the direction of Bernardo Rossellino - as regards the artistic parts, and Michelozzo who directed the architectural work.

In fact, it is precisely the external façade that was built by Rossellino's men (and Rossellino had worked closely with Alberti) in 1461; it is a very particu-

lar structure. The six Corinthian columns, instead of supporting traditional arches hold a linear trabeation, except in the central part where the trabeation curves and develops in a semicircular arch (which, built to a classic design is known as a Syrian frieze). This is an adaptation, derived from medals or ruins such as the Arc d'Orange in France, if not Hadrian's Villa at Tivoli, of a montage that had first been proposed by Donatello in the relief of the *Heart of the Miser* in Padua, made for the Altar of the Saint between 1447 and 1449. And this, perhaps was based on the front of the *Perstilium* of Diocletian's Palace in Split (and Split, like Padua was then under Venetian rule). During the same period that the Pazzi Chapel was nearing completion, Leon Battista Alberti used the same type of Syrian frieze albeit modified, on the front of the church of San Sebastiano in Mantua (1460 ca.), while the builder of the Mantuan church, Luca Fancelli was in Florence the same year.

Preceding page: *the Pazzi Chapel.* Opposite: *glazed terra-cotta tondos,* by Luca della Robbia; below: *interior of the Chapel,* facing the rectangular apse.

Preceding page: *interior view of the dome.* Above: *two polychrome tondos with the Evangelists,* by Brunelleschi.

Already from this scanty information we can assume that the portico of the Pazzi Chapel was not by Brunelleschi who never used the Syrian frieze. Nor could it be attributed to Michelozzo who never used it either, but it could have derived from the cultural ambient that revolved around Donatello-Alberti-Rossellino.

The frieze that divides the portico level from the upper level is decorated with a series of tondos with cherubs' heads attributed to Desiderio da Settignao and pupils of Donatello. While the small cupola that covers the central part of the entrance portico (pronaos) with barrel vault on the sides has glazed terracotta tondos by Luca della Robbia. Andrea della Robbia made the tondo with *St. Andrew* which is above the door to the chapel, while the elaborate bronze door leaves were made by Giuliano da Maiano.

The main architect of the interior of the chapel was the same person who designed the interior of Brunelleschi's Old Sacristy in San Lorenzo which proves Bruenellsechi's initial involvement in the Santa Croce project: two adjoining rooms, a bigger and a smaller one. To emphasize the correspondence of the four sides of the main, rectangular room in an attempt to make it look square, the large double arch turning on pilaster strips is repeated on the four walls. Between the pilaster strips on the walls there is a another series of glazed terra-cotta tondos of the *Twelve Apostles* by Luca della Robbia, while the pendentives beneath the main dome (closed in 1461) are decorated with four polychrome tondos portraying the *Four Evangelists*, and below there arc the two dolphins, emblem of the Pazzi family. The center distances between the pilaster strips are shown on the pavement through the use of different materials (white marble edging on brick red fields that Alberti metnioned in his treatise, recalling ancient Roman buildings "that were made with clay tile floors") so that it is easy to immediately perceive the proportional structure of this room while the bench that served for the basilica chapter meetings forms a sort of single base from which the pilaster strips stand out.

Preceding page: *the vault of the atrium,* by Luca della Robbia. Below, left: *stained glass window with the Pope* by Giotto; right: *stained glass window with Pontiff* by Alessio Baldovinetti, in the Museo di Santa Croce.

Bibliography

M. FRANCHI, Santa Croce, Florence s.d.

S. MENCHERINI, Santa Croce di Firenze. Memorie e documenti, Florence, 1929.

E. MICHELETTI, Santa Croce, Florence 1982.

Il complesso di Santa Croce, edited by U. BALDINI, Florence, 1983.

M. FERRARA, F. QUINTERIO, Michelozzo di Bartolomeo, Florence, 1984.

Santa Croce nell'Ottocento, Catalogue edited by M. MAFFIOLI, Florence, 1986.

S. FEI, Le vicende urbanistiche del Quartiere di Santa Croce dalle origini ai nostri giorni, Florence, 1986.

G. MOROLLI, Donatello: immagini di architettura, Florence, 1987.

G. MOROLLI, Firenze e il Classicismo. Un rapporto difficile, Florence, 1987.

Notes:
[1](p. 77) Giorgio Vasari, Live of the Artists, Vol. 1, Penguin Books, London, tr. George Bull, p.175.

INDEX

The publisher wishes to thank the Franciscan Brothers of the Basilica of Santa Croce and the "Leather School" of the Monastery of Santa Croce for their gracious cooperation.

© Copyright by Bonechi - Edizioni "Il Turismo" S.r.l.
Via dei Rustici, 5 - 50122 Florence
Phone +39-055.239.82.24/25
Fax +39-055.21.63.66
E-mail: barbara@bonechi.com
E-mail: bbonechi@dada.it
http://www.bonechi.com
Printed in Italy

Cover: Claudia Baggiani
Layout: Claudia Baggiani and Lorenzo Cerrina
Edited by: Lorena Lazzari
English Translation by: Julia Weiss
Photographs: by Paolo Bacherini for the Bonechi Edizioni "Il Turismo" S.r.l. archives
Nicola Grifoni: pp. 3, 7 (bottom), 12 (top), 15, 16, 17, 21, 24, 25 (top), 26 (top), 33 (bottom),
42, 44 (bottom), 46 (bottom), 47, 49, 50 (bottom), 51 (bottom), 52, 53, 57, 60, 65, 67 (bottom), 70 (top),
71 (top), 77, 79, 80, 83, 85 (bottom), 89, 90 91 (bottom), 92 (top),
94, 96, 97, 98, 99, 100, 101, 109 and back cover
Printed by: BO.BA.DO.MA., Florence
ISBN: 88-7204-312-3